BECOME
—AN—
IMPROVER

A CHALLENGE TO ESCAPE AVERAGE
AND UNLEASH GREATNESS

Foreword by JEREMIE KUBICEK

JUSTIN WINSTEAD

©2024 by Justin Winstead

Published by hope*books
2217 Matthews Township Pkwy
Suite D302
Matthews, NC 28105
www.hopebooks.com

hope*books is a division of hope*media
Printed in the United States of America.

First Edition
Paperback ISBN: 979-8-89185-095-8
Hardcover ISBN: 979-8-89185-096-5
Ebook ISBN: 979-8-89185-097-2
Library of Congress Number: 2024941932

hope*books
hopebooks.com
Because the world needs your hope-filled
words now more than ever

ENDORSEMENTS

Become an Improver is a tremendous resource for any individual or organization seeking to move from a place of complacency to finding purpose and meaning in life. Justin does a masterful job of explaining the barriers that we often run into that keep us from a life lived to its full potential. Through compelling stories and practical guides, he provides the pathway to building habits that will bring lasting improvement to our own lives so that we can then begin to improve the world around us.

—JEFFREY KENT, COO of Duck Commander®,
Author, Speaker

Many people find themselves drifting in life. They want things to be better, but they either stay the same or get worse. Change starts with the thinking and comes after the doing. Become an Improver is an invitation, challenge, and step-by-step process on how to rise above complacency and meaningless existence so that you can change your thinking and doing and create the life you have always wanted.

—TOM ZIGLAR, CEO of Zig Ziglar Corporation

From the first page, I was all in. Justin's genuine storytelling, mixed with actionable steps, lays out a clear path for anyone aiming to make a real impact. His mix of personal anecdotes and solid frameworks gives you a complete toolkit for improvement that's both inspiring and totally doable. If you're a leader, an aspiring influencer, or just someone who's committed to growing, this book needs to be on your shelf. *Become an Improver* doesn't just talk about change; it makes it happen.

—SKOT WALDRON, Communication Strategist, Author, Speaker, Podcast Host

This book contains so much great personal and business advice. I especially like the integration of the Christian faith with practical self-improvement ideas to be more successful and effective. We know that God provides wisdom, provision, and peace in our lives, but we also need to continually work to learn and improve. From God's promises to the transformational fable, this book is a great resource and motivator.

—SHANE BENDER, Founder of Bender CFO Services and Author of *Forecast Your Future*

I've been a leader for thirty years and can attest to the challenges the average person faces day in and day out as they try to escape the mundane rituals and challenges of the world and embrace a more excellent life. As the CEO of a faith-driven company, I recognize and value the principles, strategies, and practices outlined in this book. I encourage you to become an Improver and achieve God's full potential for your life.

—PAUL DIETZLER, CEO at *Expo Home Improvement®* **and Owner of** *Cerulean Blue Coffee House*

As a therapist, I work with clients who desperately want to unleash their greatness. I'm thrilled that with Become An Improver, Justin has given me a new therapeutic tool for my work in a book I can refer to my clients. Justin provides a perfect combination of real life wisdom through his personal hard story, and practical tools that make this book both relatable and useful. This book is a must read for anyone looking for wisdom on how to thrive as a human.

—DR. ZOE SHAW, Psychologist, Life Therapy Services, Author, Speaker

Become an Improver is a helpful examination of the things that keep us from being better. More importantly, it is filled with solutions to common challenges that leave you saying, "I can do that!". Justin has given us an honest, humble, and accessible roadmap to finally changing the things we wish were different. Real change always happens from the inside out, and Justin helps us begin that change on the inside that will produce the results we want on the outside. Winning in life requires us to win the battle of the mind, and this book makes that more achievable for all of us.

—JOSEPH BACKHOLM, Attorney, Sr. Fellow at Family Research Council, Host of *OutStanding* Podcast

As a CEO, I'm always looking for ways to improve. Justin Winstead makes improving easy with this step-by-step must-read guide.

—JUDY GAMAN, CEO, Executive Medicine of Texas and Author of *Stop Whining and Start Working*

In a world full of complacency and comfort zones, Justin calls us into an extraordinary life marked by positivity, progress, and purpose. Where others offer platitudes, this book offers concrete tools and a framework for taking action to improve your life and maximize the legacy you leave in the lives of others.

—KYLE GABHART, Author of *Legends Don't Retire and Neither Should You*, Motivational Speaker

Every day, I challenge people to find their true calling, the *thing* they were born to do. *Become an Improver* echoes that same heartbeat. This book is not just an invitation to hear about ideas but a proven process that works. The people that you lead will be grateful that you read and applied the truths in these pages. Justin has done something incredibly generous by sharing this with you, and you should take him up on his offer to become an Improver! Get a book for all of the leaders on your team so they can become Improvers together.

—TERRY WEAVER, Author of *Making Elephants Fly*, Founder of *The Thing* Conference

As I speak on stages across the country, I consistently encounter the same two questions among high-performing professionals and leaders: "How do I get better, and what will be the benefit?" *Become an Improver* answers these and will be the first book I recommend to anyone struggling with where their life currently is and hoping to make it better. Justin writes from his heart and experiences, offering practical advice to improve our lives and companies. No matter the industry, if you're a current or aspiring leader, move this book to the top of your reading list and get ready to share it with your people!

—KYLE DRAPER, Serial Entrepreneur, Author of *Rethink Everything*, Founder of Hire Culture

We can all improve, no matter how good we are or how good we think we are. Justin Winstead's new book, *Become an Improver*, is a comprehensive roadmap for progress and the ultimate guide for us all to improve ourselves every day. For those who are not yet at their best potential, *Become an Improver* will help. For those who are peak performers, you'll find lots of value as well.

—RAMON RAY, Publisher at ZoneofGenius.com,
Event Emcee, Author of *Celebrity CEO*

The depth of wisdom in this work, aligned with personal vocation, will have you on the J-curve of improvement and significance without fault. Justin's expert investment in people makes way for excellence that unlocks the limiting factors of growth and propels people into excellence, emphasizing the whole rather than the solo individual. This book will be an ageless resource for life, leadership, and legacy potential.

—TAMRA ANDRESS, Founder and President,
The Founder Collective

Justin is a master of distilling decades of lessons into stories that stick in the heart. The Improver Book isn't just a roadmap of what "to do" as a leader, it is the missing puzzle piece for how "to be." Take it slow, grow healthy, and soak in the journey. Your soul will be refreshed with the compassionate love of Jesus as you improve yourself and unleash greatness in every arena.

—SEAN KELLER, Owner of *Wilderstory*,
Executive Coach & Business Advisor

Justin Winstead's "Become an Improver" is a game-changer for anyone looking to level up in life and business. As someone who's been in the trenches of building a lasting company, I can tell you this book hits the nail on the head. Winstead's core idea of being an "Improver" resonates deeply with what I've learned over the years. It's not just about making more money or climbing the corporate ladder - it's about consistently making things better, both for yourself and those around you. What I love is how Winstead ties personal growth to business success. It's something I've seen play out time and time again: the businesses that last aren't just about smart strategies; they're built by people committed to constant improvement. This book isn't offering any get-rich-quick schemes. Instead, it's all about the long game - exactly what you need if you're serious about building something that stands the test of time. Whether you're just starting out or you've been in business for years, "Become an Improver" offers a fresh perspective that'll get you thinking differently about success. It's the kind of book I wish I'd had when I was first starting out, but it's never too late to up your game. Highly recommended! A guide to long-term, sustainable growth. Whether you're an entrepreneur or just looking to make a bigger impact, "Become an Improver" provides valuable insights and tools to help you think bigger and act more intentionally in both your personal and professional life.

—JAY OWEN, CEO at Business Builders

TABLE OF CONTENTS

ACKNOWLEDGEMENTS

This book would not have been possible without the unwavering support of the amazing people God has put in my life.

To my wife, **Kathryn**, your patience, encouragement, and belief in me have been my anchor. If not for you, I would have certainly given up long ago.

To my four wonderful children, **Jesse, Brooklyn, Abigail, and Trent**, you inspire me every day with your curiosity and boundless energy. I could not have asked for better children. More than anyone else, this book is for you.

To my parents and grandparents, your influence and sacrifices have profoundly altered my life trajectory, shaping the person I am today. I'm forever grateful.

To the original Improver Group coaching members, your dedication and steadfastness throughout the process of launching our movement and putting the Improver principles into practice have been invaluable. Your belief in our vision made this accomplishment possible.

I extend my heartfelt gratitude to my friends who offered significant encouragement and feedback along the way: **Kyle Draper, Kyle Gabhart, Kinzie Harvell, and Sean Keller**. Your insights and hands-on assistance were crucial in bringing this project to fruition.

A special thanks to the teams at **Hope Books, Improver Group,** and **Hire Culture VA** for their invaluable support in drafting, designing, editing, publishing, and distributing "Become an Improver." Your expertise and hard work ensured this book made it to the marketplace.

To my fellow **F3 Pax**, your cheers and camaraderie have been a constant source of motivation. Thank you for pushing me to be my best as a High Impact Man and for reminding me of the power of brotherhood.

Lastly, for any and all who accept the invitation to become an Improver and make the world better, I appreciate and applaud you from the depths of my heart.

I have gratitude for what is and hope for what will be.

Good and gettin' better,

Justin Winstead

PREFACE

Raised in rural Northeast Louisiana, Dad was a high-school dropout who always did back-breaking manual labor, and Mom was a public school teacher in a low-income district. Our family of five struggled to get by partially due to lower-middle-class income and partially due to a lack of financial literacy and willpower to properly manage what income we did have. One of my earliest childhood memories was looking through the floor of our mobile home and seeing the ground underneath. Our floor was damaged, and we didn't have money to repair it. The ceiling wasn't much better; when it would rain, we'd have to grab the buckets and bowls to keep the house from flooding.

As a teenager, I hated wearing my Spaldings from Walmart while my classmates sported their Nike Air Jordans. If I wanted to go on the trips with school or church, I had to be effective at the fundraisers they chose for us and learn how to sell. In high school, while my friends played sports and partied on the weekends, I worked, sweating it out in cotton fields and gins in the summers, working in retail and restaurants during the school year.

I don't know if anyone said these exact words, but there was an underlying tone among many in our rural communities: "Money is bad, rich people are evil," and if someone was successful in life or business, "They probably cheated their way to get there." The attitude towards the financially stable was a strange mix of pity and envy. Indeed, among the churches I experienced, it seemed the understanding of many that poverty was one of the greatest Christian virtues.

THE CALLING

Although our family and community may have lacked big bank accounts, we made up for it with big hearts and a lot of caring for others. Working hard and helping others was part of our DNA. Whatever I was supposed to be and do in life, I knew it would be a good, honest job. It'd be something to help other people avoid some of the discomforts and pains I had personally observed and felt.

I would help people be better and get to a better place. Already a Christian, that tug in my heart to help people be better and end up better took me toward vocational ministry. Even as a teenager, I spoke in front of crowds, officiated funerals, and led youth ministries.

Simultaneously juggling ministry, college, and working retail to pay my way through college, there was an unwelcome surprise when a lump on my neck turned out to be a cancer of the lymph system called Hodgkin's Lymphoma. While undergoing six months of chemotherapy and six weeks of radiation, I pondered deeply the meaning of life. Once in remission, I recommitted to making sure I'd live out my purpose to leave this world better than when I found it.

In 2008, I graduated college, Kathryn and I got married, and we helped start a new church (referred to as church "planting"). Also, in 2008, the world experienced a financial crisis. What timing—to be newlyweds and launch a non-profit ministry! We quickly found ourselves having lost all momentum and struggling with "nickels and noses." The money and the people just weren't there.

We merged the church plant with an existing church and soon thereafter moved to Fort Worth, Texas, to finish seminary. As soon as I had that degree, I reasoned, I could return to my mission to help people. Once in Texas, Kathryn and I began soul-searching and realized our authentic gifts and dreams did not involve us continuing in vocational ministry. We began to feel the calling for Kathryn to be a stay-at-home mom. For me, the fields of business and leadership are where I was meant to work. As one of my friends says, "God called me from *church* ministry to *business* ministry."

JUMP

The problem with me going into business was fear. I was afraid. Watching *Batman Begins*, I drew a parallel that fit my own life. As a boy, Bruce Wayne developed a fear of bats. He grew up and wanted to change the world by doing good and defeating evil. Bruce's mentor challenged him—if he genuinely wanted to be a hero, he'd have to overcome his fear...and embrace it. Bats would become a part of his identity, and he'd be reminded of his fear daily. Only then would he know his path and be the hero he desired to be.

What was true of Bruce and bats was true of me and business. As a result of things that happened in my childhood and upbringing, I was intimidated and afraid of business. The business world seemed too big and too risky. Yet, if I *really* wanted to help others, I would have to embrace it, learn it, and make it a big part of my identity. I'd become a businessman.

I decided to jump into the unknown. I would learn business, then do it well, and use it to launch me onto a platform and position to do the most good. Accepting a Fortune 500 company position in the financial services and insurance industry, I would become a student of various financial products, services, and different businesses. However, I mostly observed and learned about people.

I eventually overcame even more fear and launched my own business in the same industry. I still remember the day I left my salaried job with benefits to start my own business. My wife, Kathryn, sent this text, "Whatever we decide to do is fine with me, but we won't let fear be the basis of our decision."

Boom!

Starting from nothing and building a business from $0 income to one with millions of dollars of annual recurring revenue, taking the leap of faith began to pay off.

The problem, however, was I had become a victim of my success. On the one hand, I had healthy referral partners, loyal clients, and productive team members. My income was greater than it had ever been. There were more people in my network than ever. Everything was healthy and growing with the business.

On the other hand, every other area of my life was out of balance. In my wife's words, she "felt like a single parent for a few years." All the business lunches, happy hours, and special events had led me to pack on unwanted weight. My stress levels were up, and my morale was down. I was not learning or growing or getting better personally or professionally...I was just working. I found myself on the proverbial hamster wheel, and that was never the plan.

I wasn't fulfilling my purpose, and there definitely wasn't balance. My vague idea of goals consisted of "more and bigger." I had no specific finish line in mind, only the drive to keep running—faster. Farther. Bigger. More. I was exhausted.

LIGHT BULB

And then it hit me—it doesn't have to be this way. I decided it was time to make changes and start improving. My biggest problem wasn't lack of time, the competition, or anything to do with my circumstances; my problem was me.

— I had allowed the never-ending to-do list to drive my work.
— I chose to be reactive instead of proactive.
— I prioritized the urgent over the important.
— I played it safe with vague, comfortable goals.
— I needed to invest in myself to learn a better way.

I decided to take responsibility and own it—all of it: the successful parts of life and business and the not-so-successful parts. I was the problem, and I would be the solution.

Change is challenging; however, I knew I had to do it. Adapt and reinvent myself, again. I decided to become a student once more and learn what other successful people already knew. Then, I would do what they were doing. I hired a life/business coach. I didn't feel like I could afford it, but I did it anyway. I went to conferences. I didn't think I had the money or time to go, but I went anyway. I bought business and growth books. I wasn't motivated, but I read them anyway. I joined the mastermind group, I purchased a goal planner, I listened to podcasts and webinars. Professionally AND personally, I did whatever was required to achieve the life I desired.

Now:

- I spend less time at work while maintaining a comfortable quality of life.
- I have the capacity to take vacations and do life with my family.
- I volunteer and give back to causes I care about.
- I invest in a healthy body and healthy mind.
- I "happen to life" instead of letting it happen to me.
- I am multiplying my impact by developing leaders and teams.

I am still a work in progress and not perfect, but I have peace, abundance, and excellence in virtually every area of my life.

IMPACT

I'm living my life on purpose with a purpose. And because of that, I can encourage and influence (and minister to) others more than ever. I want more of that. I am passionate about serving others by helping them be better in their attitudes and do better in their actions so they can have more and live more.

This is why I created a coaching and consulting company and authored this book—to help individuals discover their purpose, live in excellence and wellness, and leave a legacy of greatest impact. I want to encourage and guide you to become an Improver.

I have three main goals when interacting with others in the context of improvement: enlighten the mind, encourage the heart, and equip the hands. My prayer for this book is that it will give you new knowledge and ideas, fresh encouragement and inspiration, and practical tools and systems to help you be a better person and live a better life, making a positive difference in your surroundings.

Improvement won't happen through information and inspiration from me – there must be action and transformation by you. The path to a better world begins with you. Are you ready to take the first step?

Justin Winstead

FOREWORD

Embrace the Journey of Becoming an Improver

In a world where mediocrity often reigns supreme, there exists a rare breed of individuals who refuse to settle for the status quo. These are the Improvers—those who possess an innate drive to elevate, enhance, and evolve every aspect of their lives and the lives of those around them. Justin Winstead, with his visionary perspective and profound insights, has captured the essence of this transformative journey in his latest work, "Become an Improver."

Justin's idea of being an Improver is not merely a theoretical concept; it is a practical, actionable framework designed to inspire and guide individuals in their quest for continuous improvement. This book delves into the multifaceted nature of improvement, encompassing everything from refining processes and systems to nurturing personal growth and leadership excellence. Through the lens of Justin's wisdom, readers are invited to embark on a journey that will challenge their assumptions, ignite their passion, and ultimately lead them to become agents of positive change.

For years, I have been working on creating a system of improving, knowing that when I do so others benefit greatly. As you read this book, it isn't just about you, but how daily improvements in you, can positively affect those around you.

At the core of every Improver lies an unwavering commitment to enhancing the tangible and intangible elements of the *Six Core Areas of Improvement*. Justin masterfully illustrates how a relentless pursuit of excellence in each area can transform ordinary people into "Improvers."

Justin emphasizes that improvement is not a one-time endeavor but a continuous, daily process that demands dedication, creativity, and a willingness to challenge the norm. By implementing the *Daily High Five*, you will be on your way to a life worth living.

Justin's approach to improvement is holistic, encompassing both personal and professional dimensions. He encourages leaders to engage in self-reflection, seek continuous learning, and cultivate a growth-oriented mindset. By doing so, they not only enhance their own capabilities but also inspire and elevate those they lead, creating a culture of excellence.

This book will make teams better, marriages stronger, and individuals understand their tendencies and make changes to improve.

At the heart of Justin's philosophy is the belief that true improvement extends beyond oneself. He emphasizes the importance of mentorship, support, and empowerment, sharing compelling stories and practical advice on how to uplift and inspire those around us. He challenges readers to recognize their role as catalysts for change, encouraging them to invest in the success and well-being of others, thereby creating a ripple effect of positive impact that transcends individual achievements.

Self-improvement is a lifelong journey, and Justin's exploration of personal growth is both introspective and inspiring. He delves into the importance of self-awareness, resilience, and the pursuit of continuous learning. By embracing vulnerability, seeking feedback, and committing to personal development, individuals can unlock their full potential and lead more fulfilling lives. Justin's wisdom in this area offers actionable strategies for setting goals, overcoming obstacles, and cultivating a growth mindset, guiding readers on a journey of self-discovery and transformation.

Innovation is the lifeblood of progress, and Justin celebrates the power of creative thinking and problem-solving. He explores the importance of fostering a culture of innovation, where ideas are nurtured, refined, and brought to life. His insights inspire readers to think outside the box, take risks, and drive meaningful change. By fostering a culture of innovation, we can create a future that is not only brighter but also more sustainable and inclusive.

Justin Winstead has crafted a compelling and practical guide for those who aspire to be an Improver. His wisdom, insights, and actionable strategies provide a roadmap for continuous improvement, empowering individuals and organizations to reach new heights of excellence. As you embark on this journey, remember that the path of the Improver is not always easy, but it is always rewarding. Embrace the challenge, ignite your passion, and become the change you wish to see in the world.

— **Jeremie Kubicek**, CEO of GiANT Worldwide and Co-author of The 5 Voices, 100X Leader, The Communication Code, The 5 Gears, The Peace Index and Making Your Leadership Come Alive.

CHAPTER 1

THE IMPROVER SPECTRUM

"The people who are trying to make this world worse are not taking the day off. Why should I?"
— Bob Marley

July 4, 2019, was one of the most challenging days of my life.

It started with high expectations as our group woke up to hot coffee, a warm breakfast, and a manageable segment of our 10-day, 110-mile hike around Mont Blanc. Straddling parts of France, Italy, and Switzerland, the incredible mountain range stretched our minds and challenged our bodies. This day was several days into our trek and supposed to be "the easy day."

Our plans included a short hike to a ski lift that would take us down to the quaint town of Courmayeur, Italy. There, we would enjoy authentic gelato, shopping, and sightseeing before traversing uphill to our lodging for the night. The morning went as planned until we arrived at the ski lift, which was, to our surprise, out of service. Curveball number one.

As we adjusted our plans for the day, I received an unwelcome call. My grandmother, who had been battling cancer for quite some time, had an unexpected downturn and passed away. Curveball number two.

I immediately felt the emotions of shock, sadness, and confusion all at once. This news was heart-wrenching.

There are a handful of people who have significantly altered the trajectory of my life, and "Ma Hank" was one of them. She was a special person with a wonderful knack for caring deeply about how people felt about themselves while not being concerned about what they thought of her. Not only was she a caring person, but she was also a curious one - always interested in how things work and what was on people's minds. She never let her ego get in the way of trying something new or challenging. Ma Hank would make payroll for the cotton gin repair business she ran with my grandfather, but she wasn't limited to the office tasks; she would roll up her sleeves and sweat it out while doing the dirty work.

Always putting others' needs above hers and never thinking too highly of her own image, Ma Hank consistently looked for ways to serve others. The world was a better place because of her. Without a doubt, she was someone who had a positive influence and impact on her surroundings, and Ma Hank inspired me to be that kind of person as well.

Isn't everyone on that same journey – to grow consistently and be someone who makes the world a better place?

Not quite.

While many strive to be better and improve the environments around them, many others are not making a positive difference (and might actually be making things worse). In this chapter, we'll explore what it means to live a life of positive impact and growth and discover the dangers of a negative or meaningless existence.

EXISTERS

According to Merriam-Webster, an Exister is *one who exists, observes, passively occupies space, does not affect the value of their environment.*[1]

Have you ever known someone who was an Exister? Perhaps someone at the office doing the bare minimum to get by?

In extreme examples, Existers can be like zombies, unconsciously going about their daily lives, lacking awareness or ambition. Wake up, eat breakfast, go to work, eat lunch, work more, come home, eat dinner, be entertained, go to sleep, repeat. For Existers, expressing care and concern for others is exhausting. Their best friend is apathy.

"Live and let live." They say this, but they're not actually *living* – they're just existing.

For years our family took summer trips to Destin, Florida. We would partner with a non-profit to host retreats for families with children who have cancer. On one of our trips, my wife and I were enjoying some free time at the beach while our four children played in the rolling waves of the Gulf of Mexico.

Kathryn and I would periodically check the waters to ensure our kiddos were OK. At one point, when I looked up, the kids were much farther out from the shore than we felt safe. I began to shout at them, but they were so far out they couldn't hear me.

Finally, I was able to get their attention and call them in. You can probably guess how that conversation went. "What were you doing? Why were you so far out? Weren't you paying attention?" I asked in my concerned parent's voice.

Of course, they responded that they didn't know. They were playing and sort of drifted. This sounds like the way many people live their lives—just drifting. No awareness. No intention. No purpose.

Existers live reactively. For them, life is one gigantic lazy river. Their strategy is to get the most comfortable raft and let it take them wherever it goes. They tend to make excuses and pass the blame. These people love to play the victim. Existers spend the majority of their lives being tossed to and fro by whatever is in front of them at the moment, never really taking control over their decisions.

Video game developers create dynamic characters that have a purpose in the game. The developers also design NPCs (non-player characters). The point of an NPC is to fulfill a monotonous role in the background. If you've ever seen the movie *Free Guy*, you get this idea perfectly. They're like extras for a film; filler for the important players. They are designed to be on auto-pilot and lack decision-making agency.

Many people, perhaps even you, have slipped into being an NPC in real life. Just like in video games, real life NPCs lack relevance, authority, and meaning. I don't know what your life is supposed to be about, but I do know that you should do more than take up time and space. You're more than a collection of atoms responding to chemical reactions. You were brought into existence, but not just to exist. You are made for more.

DIMINISHERS

To me, the greatest decade of moviemaking was 1985—1995. While I can't list all the blockbusters during those fantastic ten years, some of my favorites would be *Rocky*, *Top Gun*, *Indiana Jones*, *Jurassic Park*, and *Die Hard*. Although it didn't carry the same weight as those others, *Little Shop of Horrors* was a hit at the box office. For those of you who've seen it, you'll recall Twoey, who is a cross between a Venus Flytrap and a Butterwort. One of the most memorable scenes is when the crazy plant begins to sing "Feed Me" — which is the theme song of our next category of people—Diminishers.

A Diminisher is someone who takes, consumes, and drains resources and brings down the value of their environment. Unlike Existers, who have a neutral effect on their environments, Diminishers have a negative effect. Like a swarm of locusts that devour a crop, they have no regard for anything except their appetite. Diminishers are a net negative.

You've known people like this. They're easy to spot because they're always trying to push their way to the front of the line. They angle for the best seats and the first choice of food. On sports teams, Diminishers hog the ball and the glory.

I've seen Diminishers in sales environments take lead prospects that weren't theirs, badmouth their fellow team members, and lie to the customer just to get a sale. In leadership, I've seen an executive's pride bring down the value of an entire company. I've watched their ego and unwillingness to change negatively impact investors, partners, and employees.

In 2023, Robert F. Kennedy, Jr. decided to run for President of the United States. He recounted a time in his life when he was addicted to heroin for over fourteen years. He shares that he was living in "self-will" instead of "divine purpose" and that he was "just a bundle of appetites just asking to be fed."[2] This dynamic is the mindset of a Diminisher—no feeling of divine purpose, just pleasure-seekers living for their appetites.

During my sophomore year of college, I was diagnosed with cancer. As I began to grapple with this diagnosis, I connected with a couple of other guys my age who had the same type of cancer. As we compared notes, we noticed a few things in common. The most startling factor, at least to us, was that we all had some close connection with cotton fields during our teen years. One of my first jobs was "checking cotton," which is the process of examining the cotton plants for insects and diseases that could be destructive to the crop. The others also had various prolonged exposures to the fields.

As we shared our stories, we developed a hypothesis. Namely, we suspected that the pesticides sprayed on the plants by the crop duster airplanes had somehow infected us. As young teenage boys in the hot Louisiana sun, we drank out of irrigation pipes in the field. This was not abnormal—drinking out of water hoses was common back then. Years later, I remember seeing certain companies listed in a class action lawsuit for carcinogens in their pesticides.

Did a microscopic ingredient cause the potentially lethal cancer among me and the others? Apparently so. I share this story because it's a vivid reminder that it only takes a trace amount of hazardous substance to be incredibly damaging. Mental, emotional, and social poisons can cause significant harm to organizations and teams.

One example of this is gossip. A little gossip can go a long way, and Diminishers are usually behind it. Gossip is easy for Diminishers because they consistently pay attention to what's missing and what's wrong. They want more, bigger, faster...they are never satisfied. Diminishers use gossip, manipulation, and power plays to create division between teams and their leaders. They are the only ones who matter, not their company and certainly not the common good. They prioritize consumption.

Other hazards include pride, selfishness, dishonesty, lust, and greed. Even in small amounts, the effects on a person, family, team, church, or company can be devastating.

To be fair, not all Diminishers are nefarious. Some aren't intentionally manipulative, divisive, or selfish; they just lack self-awareness and struggle to do the right thing. We've likely all had someone in our lives who is hard to love. They are naïve about how emotionally draining and physically taxing on others they can be.

Patrick Lencioni's *Ideal Team Player,* is one of my favorite books on team member personalities and behaviors. He explains that the best team members possess three characteristics: humble, hungry, and smart (think: people-smart more than IQ). Those who have all three of these are ideal candidates (from a team culture perspective). However, someone can have only one or two...or none of these traits.

One of the combinations is the individual who is humble and hungry but not smart. Lencioni calls them the "accidental mess-makers."[3] Overall, these well-meaning people don't desire to do wrong, however, they leave a trail of disorder and problems in their wake. Typically, it's their lack of awareness that creates interpersonal issues. While the divider type of Diminisher is arrogant and intentional, the accidental mess-makers are awkward and accidental. Regardless, the result is that Diminishers detract value from their environment and are a net negative.

If I had to choose between being a Diminisher who makes things worse and an Exister who has no real impact, I'd choose an Exister. Thankfully, I don't have to make that choice, and neither do you. There's another option.

IMPROVERS

I was in Nashville, Tennessee, surrounded by other entrepreneurs, listening to a talk by Ian Cron on the Enneagram. I was familiar with Enneagram because I've been a long-time fan (nerd?) of personality assessments and learned the various Enneagram personality titles.

(For those who don't know about the Enneagram, it's a personality-typing system consisting of nine types divided into three unique "centers" meant to help with self-awareness and self-development.)

I had taken the assessment and knew enough to know that I was a "one." This was disappointing to me since I liked the other personality titles a little better. The ones are known as "perfectionists" (or "reformers"). Some of the other number labels were "challengers" or "enthusiasts." Both of those sounded more exciting than perfectionist. Plus, people in my past had used the perfectionist label as an insult or damaging accusation. I didn't like that title.

Ian brought relief as he explained that they had misnamed type ones. He said the more fitting title for us is "Improver."

He continued, "... They're not about making everything perfect per se; they seek to help things and people reach their potential. Improvers have a strong desire to be the best versions of themselves and make the people and environments around them better."

Little did I know how transformative this moment would be. Have you ever had one of those enlightening events where everything seems clearer and makes more sense, like the *The Matrix* red pill? It seemed like the heavens opened, and my life flashed before my eyes. I felt seen, validated, and properly characterized. Chalk one up for self-awareness.

The presentation on Improver was confirmation that for me, making myself and the things and people around me better was my reason for being on the planet. I'm not as concerned with fine-tuning every detail in my surroundings as I am with making sure there are no missed opportunities or untapped potential.

That's the real heart of an Improver—helping things and people be the best they can be. An Improver grows, progresses, and consistently improves. As we do this, we increase the value of our environments and make a positive impact on our surroundings.

DIMINISHER	EXISTER	IMPROVER
NEGATIVE IMPACT	NEUTRAL IMPACT	POSITIVE IMPACT

Remember that Mont Blanc hike I mentioned at the beginning of the chapter? It was an intense few days working to overcome the physical, mental, emotional, and spiritual challenges to complete the journey. It might have very well been impossible for me if it weren't for people who aided, supported, encouraged, and uplifted me along the way. On a micro scale, these people were Improvers. In our macro journeys, we all face our moun-tains, and we need improvers to help us along the way.

A BETTER WORLD

The world needs Improvers—people who will step up and do the difficult things, face opposition and challenges, and overcome them. As a society, much of our human existence is like a car out of alignment bent on going to-wards the ditch or oncoming traffic. Someone must step up and grab the wheel for the greater good. Someone must take responsibility and make the choice to steer. That someone is an Improver.

We have limited time on this planet, and our time here can be characterized by consuming or giving. We can be seen in the "kitchen of life" wearing a bib or an apron. The bib suggests life is about me being served, while the apron is about me serving. Do we engage others with a "here I am" or a "there you are" mindset?

In the Scripture, there are numerous examples of Jesus exhorting his followers to be the kind of people who improve society. Using phrases like "you are the salt of the earth" and "the light of the world,"[4] He illustrates the type of effects we should have on our surroundings. Salt preserves, purifies, and enhances, while light guides, en-ergizes, and protects. There is no doubt that our existence should be a net positive.

The good news is that anyone can choose to be an Improver. Although some, like myself, have natural per-sonalities (like Enneagram One) that are instinctively inclined to an Improver mindset, each person can make a decision to proactively improve themselves and the world around them. This book is an invitation for you to become an Improver.

In the pages ahead, we'll unpack what it looks like to live intentionally as an Improver and avoid becoming an Exister or Diminisher. We'll explore the six core areas of improvement, the daily habits for making life and work better, and the ongoing attitudes of an Improver. My hope with the rest of this book is to provide the mindsets and skill sets associated with improving your world. My prayer is to bring about positive change in and through you. Let's begin our journey.

(At the end of each chapter, you'll notice the sections after key points that include prompts for reflection on the good while considering direction on where to get better. I encourage you to give careful attention to these and take time to process and apply what you are learning as you go through this content.)

KEY POINTS

1. Existers live in a state of reaction. They do not create a positive or negative value and usually let life pass them. They are observers, wanderers, and drifters.
2. Diminishers actively, even if unintentionally, make things worse. They consume, divide, and damage their environments.
3. Improvers live with purpose, an unwavering aim to improve themselves and their surroundings. They go against the grain and face resistance as they pursue their calling of positive growth and impact.

QUESTIONS FOR REFLECTION (GOOD)

1. Who is someone in your *past* who you consider to be an Improver?
2. Who is *currently* in your life who you consider an improver?
3. In what areas do you positively impact others the most right now?

QUESTIONS FOR DIRECTION (GETTIN' BETTER)

1. Where do you feel like you have drifted or become an observer?
2. In what ways might others think you are an accidental mess-maker or Diminisher?
3. How could you live more in the spirit of an *Improver*?

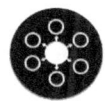

CHAPTER 2:

SIX CORE AREAS OF IMPROVEMENT

"I have... a faith in the possibility of something better. It irritates me to be told how things have always been done. I defy the tyranny of precedent."
— Clara Barton

Viktor Frankl was an Austrian psychiatrist and Holocaust survivor who would go on to author several books about the immense suffering he experienced in the Nazi concentration camps. In Man's Search for Meaning, he writes, "When a person can't find a deep sense of meaning, they distract themselves with pleasure."[5]

Frankl observed that most of those who survived the horrors of the camps had a sense of purpose or meaning in their lives. They focused on something beyond their immediate suffering, such as a loved one to reunite with, a project to complete, or a belief in a higher power.

In contrast, those lacking meaning often turned to temporary pleasures or distractions to cope with their pain. These coping mechanisms could include hoarding food, engaging in petty theft, or seeking comfort in the camaraderie of fellow prisoners. However, these distractions were fleeting and ultimately did not provide the sustenance needed to endure the harsh realities of camp life.

Although our daily life experiences do not compare to the Holocaust, Frankl's perspective is helpful when considering the way the human mind works. This feels especially relevant in our current culture, where purpose is lacking and distractions are abundant. We are faced with the choice to live with hope and meaning as Improvers or to relegate ourselves to becoming Existers and Diminishers.

In this chapter, I'll lay out Six Core Areas of Improvement and introduce practical steps for being more intentional and impactful in your journey to improve yourself and the world. These key areas are the foundational categories of making our personal and professional lives better and form the essential basis for improvement:

1. Improver of Things
2. Improver of Ideas
3. Improver of Self
4. Improver of Others
5. Improver of Teams
6. Improver of Leaders

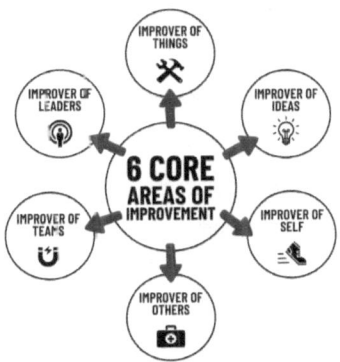

The Six Core Areas of Improvement are possible pathways for you to focus on becoming an Improver. As you reflect on how and where your life has meaning and what type of difference you might make, your journey could be any combination of these six options as you increase your growth, influence, and impact.

Each person's course is unique, and while some may be an impactful Improver in one or two of the core areas, others might hone their Improver mindsets and skill sets to make significant positive differences in all six areas. Regardless of the number or which type(s) you choose, the point of the Six Core Areas of Improvement is to be aware, focused, and intentional about becoming an Improver so we don't fall into the trap of becoming a Diminisher or Exister.

IMPROVER OF THINGS

Becoming an Improver of Things is the natural first stage for any Improver. An Improver of Things makes stuff better – food, technology, transportation, construction, science, etc. Anything related to physical matter, Improvers of Things are drawn to improve. The incredible advancements in what we see, feel, touch, hear, and taste result from someone seeing a problem or potential and doing something about it.

Improvers of things repair, restore, integrate, and innovate. They make physical things more efficient, more effective, more sustainable, more secure, and more desirable.

Have you ever seen the show "Dirty Jobs" with Mike Rowe? Every episode featured a business or organization that represented being an Improver of Things. At some level, we have each been an Improver of something, but there are those among us who have a superpower for making the tangible things in life better. We should all be grateful for the Improvers of Things.

→ *Notable Examples:* Thomas Edison, Jamie Kern Lima, Elon Musk

IMPROVER OF IDEAS

Whereas the Improver of Things focuses on physical matter, the Improver of Ideas is most at home in thoughts, concepts, and creativity. An Improver of Ideas is fascinated by the power of wonder, the potential of innovation, and the impact of transformative ideas. Working in the abstract, they chart financial plans, create building blueprints, lay out strategies, and conduct scientific research.

One hallmark of an Improver of Ideas is their ability to synthesize information from diverse sources, connect seemingly unrelated dots, and weave threads of inspiration into a tapestry of innovation. Much like the Improver of Things repairs, restores, and innovates physical objects, the Improver of Ideas refines, integrates, and strengthens mental constructs.

An Improver of Ideas breathes life into abstract concepts, infuses creativity into mundane routines, and sparks inspiration in others through their contagious passion for ideas. Where would our world be without minds like C.S. Lewis and Albert Einstein to stretch our thinking and challenge our understanding? The contributions of Improver of Ideas shape how we think, perceive, and interact with the world around us.

→ *Notable Examples:* Aristotle, Margaret Thatcher, Seth Godin

IMPROVER OF SELF

Given objects' physical and visual nature, the Improver of Things is a logical first level followed by a natural step into improving thoughts or ideas. The third area, Improver of Self, is counterintuitive, however, since we instinctively move towards attempting to enhance or refine people. We observe and are affected by people daily, and we have opinions about how they might become better with our perspective and help.

This approach is not the way. Attempting to help those around us improve before we have spent adequate time on self-awareness and self-discipline would be getting the cart ahead of the horse. Before we focus on others, we need to take a good look in the mirror. That's why this section is on becoming an Improver of Self.

James Allen wrote over 120 years ago, "People are anxious to improve their circumstances but are unwilling to improve themselves; they therefore remain bound."[6] So long as you are bound and not improving yourself, you'll be unable to improve others. Only after you have focused on your personal and professional growth to become healthy will you be in a position – practically and morally – to see how to help someone else improve.

Jesus highlighted this point in Matthew 7, where he tells a story of a self-righteous person hypocritically judging his brother. It's quite a humorous illustration where Jesus tells of the one guy who has a big log sticking out of his eye while pointing out the little toothpick in his brother's eye. (Talk about lacking self-awareness!)

Jesus says, "Hypocrite! First take the log out of your eye, and then you will see clearly to take the speck out of your brother's eye."[7] That's the core of this area, Improver of Self – becoming healthy and whole ourselves so that we can be in a position to assist others in improving.

Taking time to reflect on who we are and how we do what we do has several benefits. The first one is that it keeps us humble. Some people think the sun comes up just to hear them crow. Those people are not Improvers. Honest self-assessment can keep away arrogance and pride that restrains our ability to have a positive impact.

A second benefit of improving oneself is unlocking new possibilities. I really like this line from the classic leadership book, *See You at the Top*,[8] that states, "When you catch a glimpse of your potential, that's when passion is born." A sneak peek of our capabilities can often inspire us. Many of us get weary, not because of the tasks and work we do; our weariness results from not doing what lights a fire in us. Introspection often leads to inspiration.

The last benefit I'll mention here is that taking time to be an Improver of Self allows space for God's guidance, comfort, and conviction. When we put energy and focus on who we indeed are instead of who we want others to think we are, God speaks. We can easily spend all our time performing on the stage of life, but we should pause now and again to review our efforts and receive feedback from our Director.

The journey of personal improvement never ends, and we could discuss an infinite number of applications on the subject. In upcoming chapters, we'll pick a few of the most important as we focus on living purposefully, recognizing our potential, and maintaining integrity in our success. The shoe icon for this section symbolizes a solid foundation, a journey ahead, and taking steps to newer heights.

→ *Notable Examples:* Brené Brown, James Clear, David Goggins

IMPROVER OF OTHERS

Having started with making the things around us better, refining concepts and ideas, and moving to a state of personal improvement of self, we are now in a stronger position to serve the people in our circles of influence and help them by becoming an Improver of Others.

Improvers of Others are less concerned with changing the world and more about changing a person's world. An old story rings true about the boy saving starfish by throwing them from the beach back into the ocean. Thousands had washed up, and the boy was questioned by an older man who suggested he couldn't make much of a difference. The boy picked up another one, threw it into the ocean, and said, "It made a difference to that one."

A mentor once told me, "Do for one what you wish you could do for everyone." This quote encapsulates the spirit of an Improver of Others. They see individuals more than groups. When they hear statistics about people, they don't just listen to numbers; they imagine the individual people those numbers represent.

Matthew Perry from the hit sitcom Friends passed away while I was drafting this book, and one of his statements caught my attention:

> "I've had a lot of ups and downs in my life. I'm still working through it personally, but the best thing about me is that if an alcoholic or drug addict comes up to me and says, 'Will you help me?' I will always say, 'Yes, I know how to do that. I will do that for you, even if I can't always do it for myself! So, I do that whenever I can, in groups or one-on-one. And I created the Perry House in Malibu, a sober-living facility for men. I also wrote my play, The End of Longing, which is a personal message to the world, an exaggerated form of me as a drunk. I had

something important to say to people like me and to people who love people like me.

When I die, I know people will talk about Friencs, Friends, Friends. And I'm glad of that, happy I've done some solid work as an actor, as well as given people multiple chances to make fun of my struggles on the world wide web...but when I die, as far as my so-called accomplishments go, it would be nice if Friends were listed far behind the things I did to try to help other people. I know it won't happen, but it would be nice."[9]

Matthew Perry was an Improver of Others.

Newton's first law of motion says that a body at rest will remain at rest unless acted on by some outside force. What's true here in physical science is true in the psychological sense as well – the mind and heart of man, along with its corresponding state, absent a disruption or outside force, will remain the status quo. As Improvers of Others, we become that outside force to disrupt the lack of inertia for people and support and challenge so that their lives are better.

When it comes to helping others be better, there is a nuance that often goes overlooked. Namely, the mindset and skillset required to serve and grow others as individuals differ from those needed to serve and develop others as teams. Being an Improver of Others is about one-to-one improvement— in the next section, we'll discuss one-to-many.

It's worth noting here that all people leaders are Improvers, but not all Improvers are people leaders. Until now, we've discussed Improver of Things, Ideas, and Self, which do not necessarily involve directly managing, influencing, or leading people. The other three core areas of improvement (Others, Teams, and Leaders) deal with leading and influencing other people.

→ *Notable Examples:* Mother Teresa, Fred Rogers, Zig Ziglar

IMPROVER OF TEAMS

Improvers of Teams are among the most visible of the Improvers. Typically, front and center, they rally their people as a unit or group around a vision and goal. Experts at generating enthusiasm and buy-in, they are magnetic individuals. While the Improvers of Others are cheerleaders individually, Improvers of Teams excite and inspire their whole group or the entire organization.

Patrick Lencioni's book on the 6 Types of Working Genius[10] highlights two geniuses that are relevant to this. The Genius of Enablement is more akin to the Improver of Others, for that type of person is incredibly supportive of another person's vision and goals. They love to assist and encourage others' aspirations and often make great assistants. On the other hand, the Genius of Galvanizing is more adept at supporting the team and getting enthusiasm around a project or initiative - less about the person and more about the people. With their magnetic personalities, the galvanizing geniuses are akin to the Improvers of Teams.

I imagine a political campaign where countless volunteers and staff support the candidate by advising and assisting with background tasks. Then, the campaign staffer rallies the crowds at events, coordinates the canvassing efforts, and pioneers the get-out-to-vote initiative on election day. The former is an Improver of Others (enablement), while the latter is an Improver of Teams (galvanizing).

Improvers of Teams know how to bond others to each other and draw a team together. Their ability to command attention and affection is typically due to being fully present, inwardly strong, and outwardly kind and encouraging. This present-strong-warm combo creates a positive environment for growth and improvement.

Returning to the first area on Improvers of Things, I think about the universe and its *matter*. For the Improver of Teams, I think about the universe and its *energy*. Stars, including the sun, give energy to their environment. On the other hand, black holes are vacuums where energy and matter are "consumed." When it comes to people and their teams, individuals are typically either suns or black holes. They give energy to their team, allowing them to thrive, or they absorb positivity and progress, eventually destroying it. Improvers of Teams are the bright, life-giving stars that help unify their people and propel them to winning.

→ *Notable Examples:* Meg Whitman, Simon Sinek, Lou Holtz

IMPROVER OF LEADERS

Lastly is the Improver of Leaders. Improvers of Leaders are special people because they are willing and able to help grow someone who is already an Improver in the other five areas: things, ideas, self, others, and teams. Each of those categories requires a unique set of skills, and the Improver of Leaders can not only access what is necessary to be an Improver in those areas themselves but is willing and able to help encourage and equip others to do the same.

In many ways, when an Improver becomes an Improver of Leaders, they reach the peak of their improvement journey, especially if they are multiplying their leadership into others. While all Improvers have a positive incremental impact at some level, Improvers of Leaders have an exponential impact as they invest into more leaders. Those in this stage typically have the heaviest responsibility and the broadest reach of influence.

Benjamin Zander, the conductor of the Boston Philharmonic Orchestra, encourages people to reach their life "crescendo" not by playing the game of success but the game of contribution.[11] When you are reaching for success, it is about you. When reaching for significance (or contribution), it is about others. Improvers of Leaders desire to make maximum contributions to other key people because they want their lives to count as much as possible. They are building their legacy and seeking an incredibly significant impact.

Jesus changed the world, and there are many reasons for that. Undoubtedly, one of the most potent factors in his movement was how he invested in his core leaders. We know that thousands of people sought out his teaching and miracles, but that is not what propelled the Gospel into nations around the globe. It was his intentional method of investing in his chosen leaders. This included his disciples but even more specifically, the three he was closest to: Peter, James, and John. For all that Jesus did, the way he discipled (improved) the lives of these leaders had the most considerable ripple effect.

→ *Notable Examples:* John Maxwell, Marshall Goldsmith, Condoleezza Rice

If you wish to make the world a better place and leave a positive mark on it, playing the game of contribution and improving the lives of others is a requirement. Of course, chasing after success, possessions, accolaces, and fame are options, but that almost always leads to a life of being an Exister or Diminisher. If you want to be an Improver instead, choose your pathway from the 6 Core Areas of Improvement. Decide that you will be some combination of an Improver of Things, Ideas, Self, Others, Teams, and Leaders.

DAILY HIGH FIVE

Congratulations, you are now intentionally on the journey of becoming an Improver of _____ (whatever core areas you chose). Now what? How does one go about developing the attitudes and actions of an Improver? That's what we will uncover throughout the rest of this book through the *Daily High Five*. The *Daily High Five* represents key ambitions and practical steps anyone can take to be an Improver daily:

1. Show Thanks
2. Grow Healthy
3. Be on Purpose
4. Be Accountable
5. Serve Others

These may seem obvious and overly simple, and in some ways, they are. Yet, how often do we neglect one or more of these habits? We do so to the detriment of ourselves and our circles of influence.

Mel Robbins ignited a movement on social media she calls the "High 5 Habit," which involves giving yourself a high five in the mirror each morning when you wake up.[12] She highlights the incredible value (proven by research) of high fives for personal mental well-being and building culture for successful teams. Mel challenges her followers to implement this practice as a way of intentionally building themselves up and becoming a more positive person.

I like the idea of the High 5 Habit and feel that our daily practices would be a relevant reminder (or habit trigger) to give yourself and others a high five when you recognize one of our *Daily High Five* being observed.

For instance, you see a family member showing appreciation and gratitude—high five. You notice a team member at work exhibiting healthy accountability—high five. Someone at church makes a sacrifice in the service of others—high five. You made the decision to work through this book and grow healthy—high five!

High fives are simple, fun, and encouraging. If this book inspires people to give themselves and others high fives as they implement the *Daily High Five* practices, it will be a rescunding success in my eyes.

It's worth remembering that an Improver is one that improves themselves and their surrounding environments. Each of the *Daily High Five* is an opportunity for us to be better for ourselves and make the world better for others. In the upcoming chapters, we'll dive into each of these steps in depth and explore how you can experience positive growth, influence, and impact in an exciting and practical way.

There is more than meets the eye in the *Daily High Five*, and over the next few chapters I'm excited to share perspectives and tools with you so you can begin implementing these improvement habits and realizing their benefits immediately.

KEY POINTS

1. We can be an Improver in six core areas: Things, Ideas, Self, Others, Teams, and Leaders.
2. Improvers prioritize contribution rather than success.
3. The Daily High Five are practical steps to improving. They include showing thanks, growing healthy, being on purpose, being accountable, and serving others.

QUESTIONS FOR REFLECTION (GOOD)

1. Which area of improvement have you found most effective among the six key areas?
2. On whose life do you believe you've had the most significant positive impact?
3. In what ways have you prioritized helping others over seeking success?

QUESTIONS FOR DIRECTION (GETTIN' BETTER)

1. Which area of improvement is the most challenging for you?
2. What steps can you take to improve yourself before helping others improve?
3. How might you apply the principles of team improvement or leadership improvement in your current role or goals?

CHAPTER 3:

SHOW THANKS

"Of all the crimes that human creatures are capable of committing, the most horrid and unnatural is ingratitude."
— *Dave Hume*

Lyndon B. Johnson, when he served as the nation's Vice President, was known for his finicky obsession with the perfect heat and A/C temperature. He was particularly sensitive to the issue while aboard Air Force One, where he'd regularly engage in aggressive criticism with the flight crew, frequently insisting the cabin temperature be tweaked to just his liking.

The crew, in a stroke of genius fueled by a touch of mischief, installed a decoy thermostat in the plane's conference room. Their ruse worked. Johnson delightedly twiddled the dials, utterly unaware that his adjustments did not affect the actual ambient temperature. (It's hilarious until you realize he was responsible for the nuclear codes!)

The way we perceive reality can be an interesting (and funny) thing. This is why many say that perception *is* reality. The lens in which we choose to view our surroundings and circumstances create our understanding of what is true and affect the way we feel about ourselves and others. The word "choose" is used intentionally in the previous sentence, because we get to decide our default reaction to our environments.

A significant factor in our health and happiness is whether we choose an attitude of optimism and gratitude or allow ourselves to fall into pessimism and negativity. If you desire to be an Improver, you must begin with a humble and thankful mind and heart. As we begin exploring the *Daily High Five* in detail, we begin by being encouraged with a positive mentality and empowered with a simple method for showing thanks.

IT'S (ALMOST) ALL MENTAL

Did you know the "close door" button on elevators doesn't do anything? The Americans with Disabilities Act (ADA) that was passed in 1990 requires elevator doors to stay open for enough time that someone with a physical disability can still make it inside.[13] So those close-door buttons are just to make you *think* you have some autonomy and control. It's the same thing with crosswalk buttons in many cities, like New York City. Traffic signals are controlled by computerized patterns and are automated, so your incessant pressing is not getting you to the other side of the street any faster.[14] Here's the thing: our understanding and satisfaction with our circumstances is largely a matter of what we choose to believe

One of the admins at the middle school I attended was Mrs. Krys. She was the gatekeeper in the front office and typically the first point of contact for anyone with an issue. Mrs. Krys was famous for her "miracle mints." It didn't matter what your ailment or problem was; the red-and-white soft peppermint was her default go-to. Not feeling well? Mint. Stomach-ache? Mint! Broke your right arm on the playground? Mint!

Ok, maybe that last one was an exaggeration, but the funny thing is Mrs. Krys eliminated 80% of all the front office issues in that Jr. High with a simple piece of candy. This was possible because most of the problems 7th graders brought to the office were just mental distortions of reality. We students were choosing to see and feel a certain way and, with the help of a little sugar, could adjust our thinking quickly and magically become better.

My freshman-year psych class gave me flashbacks to this issue as I learned about the *placebo effect*. The placebo effect is a psychological phenomenon where a person experiences a real change in their health after taking a treatment with no therapeutic value—like a sugar pill—simply because they believe it will work. The placebo effect highlights how the mindset we choose has an incredible influence on the way we perceive reality.

For us to be an effective Improver, we must balance two key areas of our mindset: *contentment* and *complacency*.

Part of our human nature makes it easy to conflate these states of mind and slip into two extremes. On the one hand, we want to live in our comfort zone as much as possible. When we reach a stage in our life where the pains and problems seem outweighed by our pleasures, we can slide into complacency, which is a state of being extremely pleased or satisfied. On the other hand, some people are never satisfied. Nothing is ever good enough. The goalposts are always moving. Therein lies the struggle – reaching that sweet spot of being content but not complacent, hanging on to the good while still getting better.

G.A.G. DISORDER

It seems that part of human nature, or at least from what I've personally observed in Western culture, is that contentment is unnatural, while envy and jealousy come very naturally. A few years ago, after an extreme example of this principle on display, I began referring to the problem as "G.A.G. Disorder."

G.A.G. is short for the "Grass is Always Greener." The mental picture of gagging is gross and indicative of an underlying sickness. G.A.G. speaks to this internal rottenness, which biblically speaking is our sin nature, that we war against. The condition always sees our circumstances as deficient and lacking. We want what we don't have. Once we get what we want, we want more.

I have worked with many people in real estate, and one thing has been repeatedly proven: most people, regardless of their living situation, often think about another, more desirable home. Those in apartments believe getting a modest house will make them happy, while those in modest homes want a larger, roomier home in a nicer neighborhood. Once in the upgraded neighborhood, luxuries like home offices, pools, theater rooms, and more spaces are added to the new dream home. The wish list continues to grow. Yet, owners in the larger, upscale homes bemoan the cost, maintenance, and taxes associated with a larger estate. The upkeep and repairs on a large home can become a part-time job. Naturally, the homeowner begins to desire a smaller, more manageable house.

The same mindset for homes translates to clothing, automobiles, technology, and food. We have a natural bent towards wanting the things we do not (or cannot) have.

→ *Consider this:* Are you challenged by feelings of envy, dissatisfaction, or jealousy? If you consistently have the sense of being on the outside looking in or missing out, consider what might be the root cause of those feelings.

A friend once asked me a very convicting question, "Justin, what if you woke up tomorrow and the only things you had remaining in life were those things you felt grateful for today?"

The sting was palpable as I realized how many of my inner emotions were geared toward what I was lacking and focused on getting more instead of being grateful for what I already had, which was (and is) abundant if only I would take time to notice and appreciate.

I kid you not, my family and I were on a Caribbean cruise having dinner at one of the impeccable, upscale restaurants on board. Our main topic of discussion (initiated by me) during our meal? Where we would be having dinner the next night. (Facepalm.) Why couldn't I be fully present in the moment, appreciating the delicacy in front of me? I should have been savoring the flavors, soaking in the ambiance, and connecting with those I care about most. I should have felt contentment in that instance instead of focusing on the future and what else was to come.

I love how Dan Sullivan and Benjamin Hardy at Strategic Coach frame this concept as it relates to goals and growth. They call it "the gap and the gain."[15] Our default inclination is to zoom in on the gap between where we are and where we want to be instead of recognizing and celebrating the gains we have already made. We consistently measure ourselves against our ideal future. What we should be doing is looking at where we have been and where we are, giving attention to our progress. This bad habit of ingratitude causes us to miss meaningful moments.

Whenever my friends and I go on rucks (hikes with a weighted vest or bag), we typically comment on how refreshing it is to evaluate our progress and see how far along we've made it. Noting our progress is especially encouraging when we feel like we still have a great distance to go. We check our gains and realize we made it farther than we imagined. Suddenly, the rest of the trek feels more attainable. The recognition of accomplishment and the appreciation of our momentum propels us forward.

THE SECRET SAUCE

It's innate for the Improver to want everything to be as good as it could be and should be. We deeply value things and people reaching their fullest potential. As soon as one achievement is made, if we're not careful, there is little time to enjoy or celebrate before moving on to another endeavor.

Improvers recognize the challenge of our nature and know how to use gratitude to fuel growth.

Gratitude is the secret sauce of contentment and growth. Content people don't always have the best of everything, but they make the best of everything. This manner of viewing circumstances frees up problem-solving capabilities and activates the creative parts of our minds. The scarcity mindset robs us of these advantages. It has been consistently shown that individuals with a critical eye for detail, but an appreciation for the process and a positive outlook for the outcome will outperform the naysayers and complainers. Teams that express gratitude have higher morale, better communication, and less conflict. (After all, it's hard to be hateful when you're grateful!)

There was a poor, rural family who was greatly concerned because their little boy had not started talking. The family didn't have many resources to call upon, so the problem went on for a long time. One day, while the mother was making supper, she became overwhelmed and lost her concentration. She burned the cornbread.

After she served the meal, the little boy tasted it and hollered, "I can't eat this. It's all burned!" Shocked but happy, the mother hugged the child and asked, "Why haven't you been talking?" He said, "Up to now, everything has been OK!"

Isn't this how we are far too often? We quietly enjoy the things around us while they are pleasing, but the moment our expectations aren't met, we decide to speak up. "Constructive criticism." Sure thing, complainer.

The good news is that we can choose to be thankful. After all, we do it every November on the fourth Thursday, right? A spirit of contentment is not something that some people are born with, while others are just out of luck. We can make it a point to look back and measure the gains. We can train ourselves to celebrate achievements, both in ourselves and others. I like how Jon Acuff says, "Choose your attitude every day until it eventually chooses you right back."[16]

You can choose an attitude of thanksgiving. You can develop a habit of positive thinking and appreciation, and it's worth it to do so. The best Improvers are the ones with the most contentment.

So, how do you cultivate an attitude of gratitude? One simple technique is to imagine the opposite or (negative) inverse in any given situation. It's kind of like those old song lyrics, 'don't know what you got till it's gone."[17] Imagine that you didn't have some of the things you do have. What would your life be without food, water, shelter, clothing...Wi-Fi. (For some of you, that last word was the scariest.) We don't typically appreciate these things because they're readily available, however, their absence would be immediately and incredibly noticed.

I remember meeting Benson for the first time. He was a South African pastor turned American businessman and had a thick accent. I introduced myself and asked him how he was coing. He stopped, took a deep breath, smiled, and replied, "It's another day with free oxygen!" Benson gets it.

And it's even better than just having a spirit of thankfulness, because our principle here is show thanks. The way Benson takes his breath, smiles, and shares his words are putting his gratitude out in a way that encourages others. It's one thing to feel appreciation towards a team member, for example, but it's another thing altogether to go express that appreciation and show thanks to them. The Daily High Five practice is not just to feel and acknowledge it internally but to show thanks.

CONTENT, NOT COMPLACENT

A friend once told me an illustration of a businessman in his sedan looking at another guy in a sports car wishing it were his. A girl on a bicycle is looking at the businessman in the sedan wishing she had a car instead of her bike to get around town. An older man is walking down the street thinking how nice it would be to have a bike instead of having to walk everywhere. All of this happens while a veteran who lost both his legs in war is watching the old man walk freely on the sidewalk. No matter how bad it seems, someone else always has it worse. We can choose our perspective in our situations and decide whether we will be the victim or the victor.

Paul knew the secret...

> "I have learned to be content in whatever circumstances I find myself. I know how to make do with little, and I know how to make do with a lot. In any and all circumstances I have learned the secret of being content—whether well fed or hungry, whether in abundance or in need..."
> (Philippians 4:11-13)[18]

Paul is not talking about complacency. I am confident in saying there was nothing complacent about Paul. He was not satisfied with doing nothing and going nowhere; he had a purpose that kept him from being complacent. His last remaining goal was to travel to Spain to share the message of the Gospel where it had never been preached before. Though he was at peace within himself, he wouldn't allow himself to just exist. In other passages, Paul tells us to "give thanks in all circumstances"[19] and "give thanks for everything."[20]

Jocko Willink, a former Navy SEAL and leadership coach, has articulated a compelling philosophy that revolves around the simple word good:

> "When things are going bad, there's going to be some good that will come from it. If the mission got canceled, it's good because it allows us to focus on another one. If we didn't get the new high-speed

≥ 40 ≤

gear we wanted, it's good because it keeps things simple.

Not getting promoted? Good. It provides more time to get better.

Lack of funding? Good. We own more of the company.

Missing out on the job you wanted? Good. It's an opportunity to gain more experience and build a better resume.

If you got injured, it's good because maybe you needed a break from training.

Getting tapped out in training? Good. It's better to tap out in training than on the street.

If you got beat, it's good because you learned something.

Unexpected problems? Good. It forces you to figure out a solution.

When things are going bad, don't get bummed out, frustrated, or disheartened. Instead, look at the issue and say, "Good." Accept reality but focus on the solution. Take that issue, that setback, that problem, and turn it into something good."

Jocko's approach is not about ignoring the hard truths but about using every challenge as a stepping stone to improvement.

The bottom line here is that contentment is learning how to accept your situation for what it is and be grateful. Complacency is choosing to settle in those circumstances and reject opportunities to improve them. The Improver, learning to be content without being complacent, says, "I'll choose to see the good and appreciate my circumstances, but that doesn't mean I can't push forward on improving them."

REFLECTION AND DIRECTION

On our journey of finding the balance between gratitude and growth, I have found it helpful to pull from a couple of categories of questions. These two groups of questions are *reflection* and *direction*. For this practice, reflection is looking at your present and past and considering what is and has been, particularly the positive people, things, and events for which we can be grateful. Here you are reflecting on the good (even if it didn't feel good at the moment). For *direction*, you are looking at your present and future imagining, what could and should be improved. In other words, you are pondering what can get better.

Never taking time to review life-giving memories, relive special moments, or do an inventory of your blessings leads to resentfulness, selfishness, and a bottomless appetite. Choosing to not be intentional and responsible about what you need to improve, strengthen, and grow leads to stagnation, pride, and ignorance. In both extremes, you miss the fullness of God's grace and the opportunity to give Him glory. An Improver choosing to be content but not complacent spends time often on reflection and direction. This is a mental-emotional habit when *planning* and a spiritual one when *praying*. If you desire to immediately improve your circumstances and increase your positive influence, you can start right now by taking time to show thanks.

KEY POINTS

1. Improvers are intentional about learning to be content without being complacent.
2. Our nature is to see what's wrong and missing instead of appreciating the goodness around us; an attitude of gratitude is a choice.
3. Taking time to reflect on the good while considering what could and should get better is a healthier and more balanced approach to improvement.

QUESTIONS FOR REFLECTION (GOOD)

1. When did you experience a profound sense of gratitude?
2. Besides your family or home, what are three things that you are thankful for?
3. What are the gains that you have made recently that you haven't acknowledged or celebrated yet?

QUESTIONS FOR DIRECTION (GETTIN' BETTER)

1. What habit or system can you implement to cultivate more gratitude?
2. What do you feel is an area of complacency and "settling" in your life?
3. Who is someone you need to show thanks and gratitude towards today?

CHAPTER 4:

GROW HEALTHY

"The superior man is he who develops, in harmonious proportions, his moral, intellectual, and physical nature. This should be the end at which men of all classes should aim, and it is this only which constitutes real greatness."
— *Douglas Jerrold*

D r. John Deloney has not one, but two, doctorate degrees. He's intelligent, so when he speaks, I tune in. I remember listening to him give a talk about winning at a leadership event for entrepreneurs. I don't think he intended to single me out of the crowd, but he appeared to look me in the eye when he said, "Winning won't make you well."

I was not expecting that statement to hit home with me the way it did, but it awakened me to a blind spot. At that moment, I realized that I was inwardly counting on success – that next big deal, that next big invitation, that next revenue opportunity – to satisfy me. My sentiment was: "Once I accomplish _____, then I will be well and feel happy."

The blank was filled with ideas like being fully staffed, hitting certain revenue numbers, and having certain notoriety with books, courses, etc. If I could just achieve *that* goal, life would be easier, and I would be at peace. It's cliché, but at the time, I felt I would be made complete if I could only attain that *thing* I was missing.

For the Improver, feeling complete, or "whole," is a big deal because we put immense value on integrity. The root word of integrity is the same as integer. Math class reminder: an integer is a whole number, not a fraction. When the Improver feels divided on the inside, we are not whole and do not feel well spiritually and emotionally. We think we can fix this by getting things done, earning more money, and achieving goals, but that's a feeble attempt at treating the symptoms instead of focusing on the root issue. The priority should be on healthy growth. As we achieve goals and rack up accomplishments, we must be careful to avoid becoming a victim of our success. In this chapter, I'll show you a process for how to improve repeatedly and consistently for the long haul while keeping your wellness intact.

PRONE TO WANDER

At the leadership event I mentioned, Dr. Deloney would go on to say, "Wellness is a direction, not a destination." We don't arrive at being well. We don't cross the finish line at ultimate contentment. "Won and done, baby – I made it!" That's not the way it works.

We must intentionally and consistently put our minds toward reaching and maintaining personal health and wellness. This is true of all domains of our lives – physical, mental, spiritual, emotional, relational, etc. Sure, once we reach a certain point, keeping that level typically requires less effort, but it doesn't mean we're done.

There's a line in the old hymn, "Come Thou Fount," that says, "Prone to wander, Lord, I feel it, prone to leave the God I love."[21] We're all prone to wander or drift in life, typically towards someplace damaging or destructive. We're out of alignment and naturally bent towards a certain amount of wandering and digression. We can go from being an Improver to being an Exister or Diminisher with little effort.

This principle of human nature is not far off from the concept of entropy that states the general trend of the universe is towards death and disorder. It requires a concerted effort to keep things from breaking down, rusting, deteriorating, or slipping into chaos or confusion.

The preventative measure for us is staying intentional with our wellness. We must resolve within ourselves to become the best version of ourselves. Finding our footing and establishing stability is paramount for the Improver. When we have found solid ground, inner peace, and healthy well-being, we are in a position to dream big dreams, bring them to fruition, and repeat the process for long term winning.

SOUL CARE

We can't wish, will, or win our way to wellness. Wellness comes from wholeness. Wellness begins with becoming complete and healthy within. The connection between internal peace and external performance is stronger than many leaders would like to admit. As much as you want to win the battles *around* you, start with the battles *within* you.

Ask any salesperson who woke up feeling depressed that morning how their sales calls went later that day. Or talk to an artist about how creative they are when they've just had a conflict with their significant other. What goes on in our head and heart changes what happens with our hands. Our efforts are altered by our emotions, so we strive to get our inside right as a way of getting our outside right.

John Ortberg says, "Your soul is what integrates your will, your mind, and your body into one life." Taking care of that personal integration, that wholeness of your soul creates a stable foundation from which everything else in and around you can become better.

If you've ever done any strength training, you know that the foundation of the body is of utmost importance for overall fitness. Guys usually like to focus on the arm and chest muscles, with the biceps getting the most attention. (Welcome to the gun show, ladies!) The issue here is that many injuries have occurred when men try to curl heavy dumbbells with a weak core and bad form. They lean forward, arching their back and lifting their heels. They are not only missing the aim of their efforts (to build muscle and arm strength), but they are causing damage to the other parts of their body. All because their foundation – their feet, core, back – were not properly stabilized.

In the same way, if you don't have a strong foundation in your inner being, no matter how much you stretch, strain, and strive in the other efforts of life, you will never make the progress and experience the growth you desire. Your soul is the foundation for your personal growth. Take care of that, achieve a healthy level of peace, and you will see exponential improvement.

IMPROVER PLANNING SYSTEM

It's one thing to know the importance of being wel in life and business. It's another thing to create habits and processes that help create and safeguard your wellness. The most important aspect is to be intentional. But how exactly do you create intentionality in your winning and your wellness?

Improvers win consistently because we spend time contemplating, strategizing, and ideating about what is to come. We love living in the future! Once there is a vision or goal with a plan, healthy Improvers take steps toward completion, periodically reviewing progress, and celebrating gains. After a project has been completed, a habit has been implemented, or an achievement has been attained, Improvers have a rhythm of recharging and resetting that allows for more success.

These "reflection and direction" rhythms create optimal health when done quarterly, monthly, weekly, and daily. At our company, *Improver Group*, I have organized these cycles into our *Improver Planning System*. Our model is based on proven principles for being effective and productive with your focus and effort. The process is meant to help you be the architect of your vision and goals by creating your blueprint for growth and success while building and maintaining internal wellness along the way.

There is an acronym by church growth expert, Nelson Searcy, that is relevant here as he says a S.Y.S.T.EM.[22] saves you stress, time, energy, and money. It is possible to live a happy and healthy life apart from the *Improver Planning System* or other similar programs, but chances are it will cost you stress, time, energy, and money. Learning and implementing this process is a front-end investment that will yield a back-end return.

Could you imagine being a captain of a ship without charting your course? What about being a chef without a menu? Or a teacher without lesson plans? These examples are what it's like trying to be an Improver without a planning system.

If you are feeling frustrated or discouraged in the pursuit of your goals, especially connected to your wellness, it's likely you're just winging it. Or, as grandmother used to say, "You're flying by the seat of your pants." With this manner of working and task management, growth, influence, and impact will always be limited. The *Improver Planning System* is your answer, as it helps you become more proactive and efficient with your talent and treasure investments.

In the upcoming sections, I will identify the most vital parts of the *Improver Planning System* along with sample excerpts from our *Improver Planner*, which is the print tool version of our process. While the *Improver Planner* isn't required for you to efficiently achieve goals, the core components of this philosophy and process are. The main elements of the quarterly process include: quarterly planning session to map your vision and goal details, monthly action plan, weekly reviews, and daily actions.

QUARTERLY PLANNING SESSION

I find it interesting that every year there is a three-month cycle that begins in November with a focus on thanksgiving and gratitude. Then, in December, there is an emphasis on celebration, giving, and peace, followed by a focus in January on new beginnings, fresh starts, and hopeful goals. I believe a 90-day period that essentially consists of being intentional in gratitude, giving, and growth is a good cycle to repeat throughout the year. I recommend Improvers follow these three stages every three months because it puts us on a cycle of doing quarterly what many people only do annually. The cadence of this habit, which I refer to as a *Quarterly Planning Session*, is an advantage that empowers us to be better more consistently.

For the *Quarterly Planning Session*, I suggest starting with up to 5-7 important goals you would like to accomplish over the next 12-18 months. Asking questions like, "What accomplishment would help me become closer to my desired future?" or "What achievement would make everything else easier or better?" or "What goal, if completed, would increase the chances of winning with my other goals?" Once you have this list of goals, you will choose 1-3 goals to begin focusing on this quarter. If you complete one of those goals, you can begin another one. Whatever goals are incomplete from your original list, you can move on to the next quarter.

FAST GOALS

Many people use the SMART[23] goals framework or some variation of it for writing their goals. However, I train aspiring high performers to create FAST goals. The idea of *fast* reminds me how important taking quick action and creating momentum is for moving forward on your vision. (Bonus points for those who *fast*, as in abstaining from food/drink and spending time in meditation/prayer, in the process of developing or working towards your FAST goals!)

The components of a FAST goal are:

Front-and-Center – You need to have them printed and visible to you often (at least daily). This can be as simple as a written list on notebook paper or as elaborate as you like. The main thing is putting the words down and letting them be a consistent reminder. (Be careful of digital lists that get created and filed away, never to be seen again.)

Accountability-Based – Your goals should be crafted such that someone can easily hold you accountable, and you share your goals only with those who can encourage you and keep you on track for achievement.

Specific – Your goals need to clearly define what crossing the finish line looks like. There should be a clear from x to y change indicated in your goal. If there is ambiguity around what winning looks like, keep working on it.

Time-Bound – You must set a deadline for your goals. It's human nature for our focus and efforts to expand and contract based on the time allotted. Set a reasonable deadline and work to complete it ahead of schedule.

Goal examples:

Typical: I hope to read more.
Improved: I will read two books per month this year.

Typical: Increase sales and revenue.
Improved: Our team will achieve new business sales growth of 25% by the end of Q3.

Typical: I want to lose weight.
Improved: I will lose 15 lbs. by May 31st.

Typical: Hire more staff.

Improved: We will hire an assistant, two support personnel, and four sales team members in the next 90 days.

GETTING CLEARER

Once you have your list of FAST goals, for optimal clarity and conviction, you should break them down into even greater detail. There are six key areas I define when setting goals: vision, motivation, action, opposition, completion, and celebration.

Vision

What is my desired outcome? As you imagine your hopeful future, consider the changes that must take place. These gaps in where you are and where you desire should be broken down into manageable chunks. The main "meat" of your FAST goal is what goes here.

These micro-visions are your goals and typically fall into eight key categories of growth: mental, financial, spiritual, recreational, physical, relational, professional, and missional. Almost any worthwhile ambition falls within these labels. By selecting these categories in the goal planning process, you are able to visualize a more balanced approach to your ambitions. Are you only focused on one or two areas, like financial or physical, each time you set goals? Most people naturally lean towards certain of life's domains while unknowingly avoiding the others. Ideally, your overall vision will be a well-rounded one with success in all the key categories of life.

Motivation

What do I hope improves by reaching this goal? The completion of your goal should make you and/or your environment better. Consider the positive impact of your goals. Sometimes, we call this your "inner why" or your "noble reasons." People usually list things like "leave a meaningful legacy," or "make a difference in my community," or "be a healthier version of myself." It's the big idea picture of your why.

Action

What significant milestones will help me achieve this goal? Some people confuse goals and projects. If goals are finish lines, projects are the steps – the tasks and actions – that help us get closer to completion. Think of the practical, actionable items that you can begin immediately. Perhaps counter-intuitively, the smaller and more attainable the step, the better. Creating momentum through micro successes is a hidden gem of success. This list of action isn't meant to be comprehensive, but a start on the natural next steps to create positive movement.

Opposition

What obstacles will I need to overcome? Accomplishing anything meaningful requires perseverance and tenacity. There are risks and potential problems in our endeavors, and the Improver learns to anticipate them, then overcome or avoid them.

Completion

What is my deadline? You should identify a due date and attach it to your goal. There is power in impending events and knowing whether you are on pace for success.

Celebration

How will I reward myself? You may not think you need to celebrate or reward your wins, but your subconscious appreciates the affirmation and will support your next goal. When you take risks, make sacrifices, and work hard to accomplish a goal, you need to enjoy the fruits of your labor. Mark the moment with something that excites you.

Note: The text for your FAST goals should match what you indicate in your *vision* and *completion* portions.

The point of this exercise is to illuminate the *what, why, when,* and *how* of what you are striving to make better. Time and effort here result in direction and speed later.

MONTHLY ACTION PLAN

Now that you have your list of goals clearly defined and organized, you can begin thinking about your most important objectives broken down by month. There are two primary areas I think about with our Monthly Action Plan:

Milestones – What will I accomplish this month?

This is where you list specific projects or big tasks you need to complete over the next 30ish days to move forward on your goal. The difference between this and the goals are that the projects are the key stages of progress leading toward your larger goal. Using the imagery of a marathon runner, the finish line is the goal, and the milestones are the progress mile-markers along the way.

Accountability – Who will I enlist to encourage me?

As your goals change, your support system may change as well. Think about who will partner with you for accountability each month. Share your immediate goals with them (either in FAST format or the Goal Details) and request their support and challenge. And get ready in chapter six for helpful tips on being accountable.

WEEKLY UPDATE

Perhaps the most important rhythm of the *Improver Planning System* is the Weekly Update, which is really a time of looking back and looking ahead. Here, you're spending time glancing at the rear-view mirror from the past seven days while also peering through the windshield for what's coming up. The review section is where you will look back at your achievements and results. You'll follow this with intentional gratitude.

After you have taken time to review the prior week, you'll preview the upcoming week. The preview is identifying your opportunities for growth and improvement and listing your to-do's and to-be's. In other words, to make progress on your goals, what tasks must you accomplish, and what attitudes or mindset should you embody?

The prompts for this weekly ritual are:

Results – What were my biggest wins from this past week?

Review – What progress did I make on my milestones this week?

Reflect – What am I grateful for this week? Take time to be thankful. Think:

○ What good happened TO me?

○ What good happened THROUGH me?

Reward – Who requires recognition and appreciation?

Refocus – Where can I direct my efforts to grow and improve in the coming week?

To Do (Action) – What are the top three milestones I should strive towards this week? These milestones are key moments or events leading up to the achievement of my quarterly goal(s). Up to three milestones per week are listed with some of the tasks attached under them so that the immediate next steps towards completion are clear.

To Be (Attitudes) – What attitudes or mindsets must I embody this week? Some weeks, you need to be more focused, while others are more restful. Perhaps this week, you need to be mostly creative and strategic, whereas next week, it's about being generous and patient with others. There are endless possibilities here, which is why we included a blank in our planner under this section. The key is thinking through not only *what* you need to do but *how* you will do it.

These reflection and direction questions may seem daunting at first, but it only takes a few times to hit your stride. This process typically only takes me less than 20-30 minutes to work through each week. I have found the best time for me to do the Weekly Update is every Sunday afternoon or evening, but you will need to find what works for you. The important thing is to take time each week to review your prior week and preview your upcoming week.

DAILY ACTION

Like the weekly rhythm, you should set aside a time block each day to think about your "To Do" and "To Be" objectives and two reflection questions. This is your daily habit of being intentional and proactive with your time, focus, and energy.

> *To Do (Action)* – What tasks must I accomplish today?
>
> *To Be (Attitude)* – What attitudes or behaviors must I embody today?
>
> *Reflect on Good* – What am I grateful for today?
>
> *Reflect on Gettin' Better* – What improved today?

The average person does a status check on several things daily: weather, mail, stocks, social media, electronic messages, etc. Additionally, we look in the mirror and check the time several times throughout the day. The Daily Tasks can and should become a part of that rhythm. In a world of distractions, it will keep you on track, focused, and productive.

QUARTERLY REVIEW

After you have implemented these steps for about thirteen weeks (or three months), you are primed for a Quarterly Review, which is an essential part of your *Quarterly Planning Session*. We already highlighted the importance of a ninety-day gratitude-to-growth rhythm, so here we'll just focus on the core stages needed for assessing and adjusting for improvement.

Results – What were my biggest accomplishments this quarter?

Review – What was my goal progress this quarter?

Reflect – What am I grateful for this quarter?

Reward – Did I celebrate my achievements?

Rest – Did I take time to rest and rejuvenate?

Refocus – What are my goals for next quarter?

Recommit – What steps do I need to begin taking?

LOST IN YELLOWSTONE

My wife and I took our four children to explore Yellowstone National Park one summer, and what an adventure it was. The sights, smells, and sounds there are beyond description, and the experience of observing bison, wolves, bears, elk, and other animals was equally interesting and intimidating. One of our more exciting excursions was a several-mile hike into one of the more remote and hidden areas of the park. Thankfully, we had our AllTrails app and national park signage to point us in the correct direction.

Somewhere along the way, however, we realized we were no longer on the right track. The path looked different; the directional signs were apparently gone, and it had been a while since we had seen other hikers. To make matters worse, we were out of cell signal range, so our free version of the AllTrails app wasn't working, which meant we were navigating on our own.

Being several hours into our hike and not remembering all the twists and turns that led us to where we were, a slight bit of concern began to build. The sun was starting to set, the temperature was dropping, and the images of the wolves and bears were starting to permeate my mind. I did not have the provisions to provide for and protect my family overnight, and the realization that I had put us all into danger was a mix of anxiety, frustration, and embarrassment. But, as all successful leaders know, you can't let fear, stress, and uncertainty keep you from moving forward, so that's what we did. One step at a time, we pressed on.

After a while of walking (and worrying), we noticed a couple of trail markers. There was a little hope and relief. As we continued, we came to realize that we had unknowingly drifted off the hiking trail and onto the equestrian trail in that section of the park. This misstep led to our disorientation and confusion about where we were and where we needed to go next. Even still, the small colored markers soon gave way to signs with distances and directions, and we were on our way to safety. Whew!

Every time I think about vision and goal planning, I am reminded of that experience in Yellowstone. Just as with the hike, our personal and professional ambitions start out with anticipation and excitement, imagining the adventure and fun we will have. But it doesn't take long before our journeys are thwarted by disruptions and distractions that knock us off our path. We can easily become lost. Sure, we might still be moving, but there is worry and concern about the direction of our activity and whether our efforts are taking us to a place of safety and comfort.

What we need is a trail map to guide our steps. We need mile markers and indicators along the way, letting us know we're on the right track. That's what the *Improver Planning System* is intended to do for you - give you the direction, affirmation, and clarity you need so you can have an amazing adventure without putting yourself in dangerous situations or in circumstances that steal your joy.

IMPROVERS GROW HEALTHY

Just like any new habit or process, it takes time and effort to implement this planning system and get comfortable with it. But, it's just like walking – feels awkward at first and there are lots of mistakes and missteps, but once you get the hang of it, everything else is easier and better! Proverbs 21:5 instructs us, "If you plan and work hard, you will have plenty..."[24] Healthiness, wellness, and plenty comes from planning well and working hard.

For anyone wanting to be an Improver, which is to grow themselves and increase their influence and impact, these rhythms are vital. It's possible to accomplish goals and win without all the elements in the *Improver Planning System*, but it's incredibly difficult and highly unlikely that you can sustain success long-term in all the key areas of life and business without consistently practicing these habits.

Becoming clear, focused, and disciplined in execution guarantees you healthy growth and consistent improvement for a lifetime. Having a system of your goals will save you stress, time, energy, and money over the long haul. The Improver doesn't just want to grow in an unhealthy, unsustainable manner, and likewise doesn't want to just maintain current level of health. The Improver desires wellness and goes through the prayer, planning, and practice necessary to grow healthy each day.

KEY POINTS

1. Simply winning or accomplishing goals does not result in wellness.
2. Our nature is to become distracted and discouraged, to wander and drift.
3. Healthy growth over the long haul requires intentional habits of reflection and direction.

QUESTIONS FOR REFLECTION (GOOD)

1. What is the most meaningful goal you have ever achieved?
2. What habits are currently helping you get things done?
3. What profound change have you successfully made in your life?

QUESTIONS FOR DIRECTION (GETTIN' BETTER)

1. In what area of your vision and goals are you unclear or unfocused?
2. How can you improve your process of looking back and looking ahead?
3. Are there achievements for which you need to express gratitude or take time to celebrate?

CHAPTER 5:

BE ON PURPOSE

"There are two great days in a person's life: the day we are born and the day we discover why."
— William Barclay

You may have heard the story of the little boy who once made quite the scene at a wedding. He walked down the aisle, and as he made his way to the front, he would take two steps, stop, and turn to the crowd, alternating between the bride's side and the groom's side. While facing the crowd, he would put his hands up like claws and roar. And so it went step, step, ROAR, step, step, ROAR- all the way down the aisle.

As you can imagine, the crowd was near tears from laughing so hard by the time he reached the pulpit. The little boy, however. was getting increasingly distressed from all the laughing, and he was near tears by the time he reached the pu pit. When asked what he was doing, the child sniffed back his tears and said, "I was being the ring bear!"

The way we see ourselves and our purpose determines our actions and behaviors. The boy's misunderstanding of the difference between ring "bear" and "bearer" led him to behave in a way that was unintended and resulted in embarrassment. In a similar vein, many people strive unsuccessfully to change their behaviors, routines, and habits without changing their identity. As it is well known, our nature does not allow us to consistently perform in a manner which is inconsistent with the way we see ourselves. The perspective you have about your identity and purpose internally shapes what you do externally.

As a preteen, I was getting a little too big for my britches, and I remember my mom asking me incredulously, "Who do you think you are?" The idea of this chapter is to ask you the same thing: who do you think you are? What is your purpose?

In the last chapter on growing healthy, you were challenged to live intentionally and set goals to help you create wellness and be productive with your time, focus, and effort. The "Be on Purpose" step of the *Daily High Five* is to make sure those activities are in line with your larger life vision purpose(s). To be an Improver is to know who we are and what we're meant to do and spend our lives striving to live that out. The importance of the following content is paramount to bringing your desired future to reality and achieving a life well-lived.

INSIDE-OUT

When I compare most of the religions of the world with Biblical teaching, I notice a stark distinction. The other religions start with the rituals and rules that you are to follow. With enough adherence and discipline to their prescriptive practices, you will change as a person over time and earn some reward. It's an outside-in approach.

Jesus, on the other hand, blasted the religious leaders of his day for cleaning up the outside of the cup and dish while the inside was still filthy. When He would engage with people, He would do things like touch a lady who had been considered "unclean" (due to a prolonged bleeding disease) and call her "daughter." When Peter first encountered Jesus, he was nicknamed "Cephas," which means stone or rock. He told the Pharisee Nicodemus he must be "born again." When pressed on this, Jesus explained it was an internal, "spiritual rebirth," not a physical one. The foundational truth of the Gospel is that by grace, we are forgiven first. Then, because of that new identity, we follow. God prioritizes the intrinsic value and identity of a person over external behaviors.

Growing up in the church world I would always hear people say things like, "I'm just a sinner saved by grace." I understand their sentiment and agree with it to an extent. Theologically, they were not technically wrong. The challenge is that the descriptor "just a sinner" was their primary identity, and the result was they walked under that self-image typically justifying their continued sinful habits.

The Scripture teaches that when we are *justified*, we become a new creation, a member of the family of God, enlisted in the army of God, one of his saints, and joint heirs with Christ. We are put on a mission to enjoy his goodness and share his glory with the world. If you embrace that identity and purpose, it changes the way you spend your focus, time, money, and energy. It's an inside-out approach.

For the Improver, we must see ourselves in this light, as agents for good. We are catalysts that make things better. Our identity as Improvers will lead us to behave more positively and strive for progress. One of the goals of this book is for you to embrace the label of an Improver. I believe that if you see yourself as a driving force for worthy endeavors and a net positive on your environment, your behavior will reflect that identity.

I hope that hiring managers, when considering a candidate for a job, will evaluate whether the applicant is an Improver. Much like we describe certain people as being a "leader," in the future I hope people will be labeled as an Improvers. (After all, all leaders are Improvers, but not all Improvers are leaders.)

High achievers who aim to carry the identity of Improvers have visions that are bigger and more outward-focused. Instead of being driven by purely selfish motives like the Existers and Diminishers, Improvers set goals that lead to win-win scenarios and bless more people than themselves. In the quest to do good, Improvers live and work with positive intentionality knowing that is in line with who they are.

RUN, FORREST, RUN

Remember the scene in Forrest Gump where Jenny leaves him, and he begins to run? You feel the emotions that drive him to leave. However, somewhere along the way, he finds himself running incessantly for no clear reason. He does this for three years, two months, and 14 days. When asked why he was doing it, he responded, "For no particular reason." (You read that phrase in Forrest's voice, didn't you?)

Coaching individuals and teams for years, I have noticed a pattern where people start at the beginning with a strong emotion and desire, but somewhere along the way, they wake up and they're doing their routines "for no particular reason." They just do what they do without much thought. Not quite a zombie level but getting close.

Thomas Merton, the prolific American monk and writer, pointed out that we may spend our whole life climbing the ladder of success, only to find when we get to the top that our ladder is leaning against the wrong wall. My friend, don't spend your life racing up the ladder not even thinking about where it's taking you. This is not a race against other people and their ladders. And lifehacking away from your purpose just gets you to the wrong destination faster. Don't be a Forrest and just run without the end in mind. Discern where your ladder should lean and intentionally climb it at your pace.

DISCOVERING YOUR WHY

What if you do not know your purpose? Many people struggle with knowing if they have a purpose and, if so, what it might be. To help people realize their "why" and gain direction in their life and work, I have used a diagram with exercises I call the Personal Purpose Tool.

The Purpose Tool begins in three key categories:

— Passions & Proficiencies
— People & Places
— Pressures & Problems

As we look at each of these, if you are seeking clarity on your purpose, I'd encourage you to take note of your thoughts.

Passions & Proficiencies

First, consider the types of activities and work you enjoy most. This is your area of passion. Reflect on what excites you, the kind of work that feels fun and brings you energy and joy. This one can be tricky because sometimes we don't know we're passionate about a thing until we're skilled at it. But there are usually types of activities that we know bring us positive energy when we're working on them. Additionally, you can probably think of things that give you a sense of accomplishment and satisfaction when they're completed.

Proficiencies are those functions in life and work that you naturally excel in, unique giftings that are a part of what makes you, you. These typically fall into two categories: soft skills and hard skills. Soft skills are qualities, attitudes, and characteristics about you. Hard skills are talents and abilities that you bring to the table. Some of your skills are a result of choice, but some are part of your nature – they're in your DNA. Consider all hard skill and soft skill areas you are proficient in.

People & Places

Now that you have where you find enjoyment and excellence, you must decide whether there is a possibility to bring it to market. That's the people and places circle. Here, we're considering whether there are individuals to offer your product or service that would allow you to sustain doing it long-term and where they are. It's a rather unfortunate reality, but sometimes the things we enjoy and can do well don't meet a real need in the market. When we find ourselves in that situation, what we have is a hobby or a charitable cause, but it's not our purpose.

You must consider where there are opportunities for meaningful results and win-win situations. This may require data research or asking around for perspective. It may be that you have an incredible offering that energizes you, but the place you're currently in is not a fit. This could require moving to a new position, company, or industry. You may have to change homes, churches, or memberships.

Additionally, God may have given you a burden or excitement around a certain group of people in a different city, state, or country. Include all the places and people groups that surface in your mind, especially if you have a strong conviction for them and feel you could serve them well.

Pressures & Problems

The third circle is "pressures and problems." What you'll want to do here is reflect on the pain points you've experienced in the past and are particularly sensitive to or interested in. What are the challenges that you have overcome and desire to help others conquer? Often, your mess becomes your message, your pain creates your platform, your hard struggle fuels your powerful story, and your crisis confirms your calling. Simply considering what people are dealing with and how you might help them find hope, healing, and joy can bring clarity to your purpose.

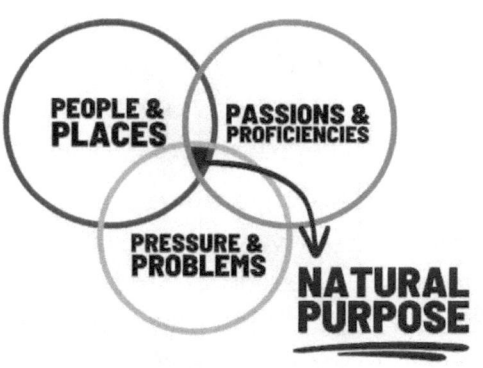

NATURAL PURPOSE VS DIVINE PURPOSE

If you were to stop here, you would have gained a lot of ground in understanding the potential areas of purpose for your life. It's possible to explore these three areas from a purely logical, naturalistic understanding of the world and conclude with a purpose that would be adequate for a relatively happy life. Certainly, many people have found satisfaction by aligning their talents and passions in a way that meets the needs and desires of others.

I refer to this as your *natural purpose* in that it is an intuitive, practical approach to living life. Your natural purpose is self-determined by reasoning through your thoughts and factoring in your feelings on what you ought to do. Working and living in your natural purpose, when done well, can be an efficient and effective way to exist. I contend, however, that we are to be more than Existers. We are meant to be Improvers, and there is a higher level of purpose to which we should aspire.

Remember in grade school when we were asked: "What do you want to be when you grow up?" It's the wrong question. My plans in life should not consist of what *I want to be*. The better question is: "What do you think God's called you to be when you grow up?"

The answer to that question is your *divine purpose*. Your *divine purpose* is your divine calling, predestined before the universe was created. From a Biblical perspective, everyone has a predetermined reason for their existence, a divine purpose. You might also call it a providential purpose. You have a special *mission* and a unique *message* the world needs.

The Scriptures tell us that we are "awesomely and wonderfully made," that we are "skillfully formed," and "our days were ordained" before they even began.[25] Additionally, "... we are God's masterpiece. He has created... so we can do the good things he planned for us long ago."[26] Many in our society suggest that you *determine* your purpose, while I argue that we *discover* our purpose.

Proverbs 20:5 tells us that "many are the plans in a person's heart, but it is the Lord's purpose that prevails."[27] We have our plans, of course, but God knows his purpose for our lives. And it's our responsibility to uncover it and live it out. To find our divine purpose, we seek our

Designer and strive to understand what He intended our role to be. I believe you can and should unlock your real mission in life and find your divine purpose. You start by taking inventory of your natural purposes, then reflecting on God's *promises* and responding to His *pull*. These next two sections will unpack how we engage with God on this journey of discovery and fulfillment.

Promises of God

There is incredible power in reading and meditating on the promises God has made to his people. The five types of promise that are included here are just a sampling of the encouragement Scripture offers to the Believer who is seeking God's will for his or her life. These areas of promise are provision, peace, protection, power, and presence.

— **Promise of Provision** - *God will provide for your needs.*

"And God will generously provide... everything you need and plenty left over to share with others."[28]

"Don't worry about your life, what you will eat or what you will drink; or about your body, what you will wear... your heavenly Father knows that you need them. But seek first the kingdom of God and his righteousness, and all these things will be provided for you."[29]

— **Promise of Peace** - *God will give you hope and a calm inner spirit.*

"Don't worry about anything, but in everything, through prayer and petition with thanksgiving, present your requests to God. And the peace of

God, which surpasses all understanding, will guard your hearts and minds in Christ Jesus."[30]

"I am leaving you with a gift—peace of mind and heart. And the peace I give is a gift the world cannot give. So don't be troubled or afraid."[31]

— **Promise of Protection** - *God will rescue you from danger.*

"But the Lord is faithful, and he will strengthen you and guard you from the evil one."[32]

"And we know that in all things God works for the good of those who love him, who have been called according to his purpose."[33]

— **Promise of Power** - *God will strengthen you to endure and overcome.*

"But he said to me, 'My grace is sufficient for you, for my power is made perfect in weakness.' Therefore, I will most gladly boast all the more about my weaknesses, so that Christ's power may reside in me."[34]

"Now to him who is able to do immeasurably more than all we ask or imagine, according to his power that is at work within us."[35]

— **Promise of Presence** - *God will be with you, and you will know Him.*

"And I will ask the Father, and he will give you another advocate to help you and be with you forever—the

Spirit of truth...you know him, for he lives with you and will be in you."[36]

"God has said, 'Never will I leave you or abandon you.'"[37]

These verses are a small sampling of the Scriptures that speak of God's promises, but as you work through the process of discovering your divine purpose, consider which of these promises has the most meaningful encouragement for you. This will bring clarity to your journey of discovering your divine purpose.

→ *Consider this:* Which of those promises give you the most encouragement right now?

Pull of God

When we make decisions, we can easily forget to include God. We pull out the spreadsheets and make logical calculations based purely on what we're good at and enjoy and where there seems to be a market for our gifts, services, and products. I think it's a good idea for that to be a part of our decision-making system, but it should be balanced with where God is pulling your inner spirit.

Sometimes, our feelings deceive us, but often, our instinct or our "gut," is guiding us towards the right path. This internal inclination, for the Believer, can be God pulling us one way or the other. People struggle with knowing God's direction, and I don't claim to know the mind of God. However, I have applied four steps to hearing his voice that have been significant in my life:

1. *His Spirit* – Where do I feel his Spirit leading my inner spirit? As we meditate and pray, we must consider what we believe his voice is speaking to our hearts and minds.
2. *His Word* – In the same way we reflect on his promises found in the Bible, we also consider what his instructions and proclamations are. What do the Scriptures say? God will never lead us to do something contrary to the truths of his Word.
3. *His People* – God speaks through wise counsel. He puts people in positions of experience and authority so they can speak truth into our lives. Seeking advice and encouragement from our mature brothers and sisters in the faith is always recommended.
4. *His Sovereignty* – God often aligns circumstances and situations in a way that is indicative of where he is leading. Some things are too coincidental to be accidental. Unexpected obstacles and opportunities give us clues to where God is working. Being aware of the doors he is opening and closing can provide context to where he is pulling.

It has been my experience that when I seek how and where God is leading in *all* four of these methods, I have taken the right path and made the wisest choice. When basing my decision on one or two of these steps, I am prone to error and sometimes get off track. For example, I might misinterpret the Bible (his Word) or take passages out of context. Or my friend (his people) may give me bad advice. I could misread situations and circumstances (his sovereignty) or mistake my emotions for God's voice (his

Spirit). Individually, these indicators might point me in the proper direction, but there is still risk of being confused or making the wrong decision. Yet, when all four of these pull categories indicate the same pathway, it gives me peace of mind and assurance that I am being directed by God. I feel certain that if you are seeking God's plan for your life, and his Spirit, Word, people, and sovereignty are all pointing in a specific direction, your divine purpose will be much clearer.

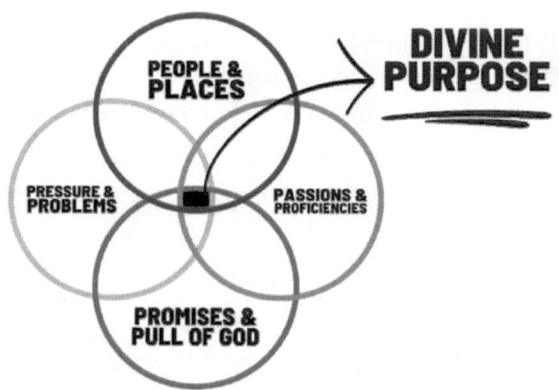

(Some of my Christian friends have argued that the *Pull of God is* the only one of these factors that matters and that we should focus only on the *pull* part of the equation. However, I have found that spending time reflecting and listing out the variables in the other circles untangles the web of conflicting thoughts and emotions we face when attempting to understand God's assignment at any given time. One of my mentors used to say, "Don't let what you *don't* know rob you of what you *do* know." It's a best practice to start with what you do know as you seek God for those things you don't know, including your purpose.

In this context, identifying passions, proficiencies, problems, etc., provides clarity and lays a strong foundation for the *Pull of God*.)

YOUR SWEET SPOT

There are few feelings better than knowing that you are where God wants you to be, doing what God wants you to do for the people he's called you to help. Ken Coleman says, "Your sweet spot is where your greatest talent and your greatest passion intersect."[38] I like that statement a lot and feel like we can elaborate on it by saying,

> **"You're in your sweet spot when God pulls you to a place where your greatest talents and passions intersect in a way that helps people with their pressures and pain points."**

The clarity here is that your sweet spot isn't primarily about you; it's about God's mission for you to serve others.

When you choose to live a life of intentionality and purpose, others will take note. This can't be some forced caricature of who you think people want you to be. The world needs the you that you were created to be. A clear purpose will help you avoid distraction, division, and discouragement. Discover and embrace your divine purpose in life, and not only will you be better, but the people in your circles of influence will be better as well.

KEY POINTS

1. Our self-perception and understanding of our purpose shapes our attitudes and behaviors. We are inconsistent with our activity when we are confused about our identity.
2. Our natural purpose can be found by identifying where our desires and abilities meet practical needs of others, while our divine purpose goes deeper by exploring the promises and pull of God.
3. Once we have our purpose defined, Improvers live intentionally prioritizing our efforts and tasks for maximum impact.

QUESTIONS FOR REFLECTION (GOOD)

1. What do you already know about your purpose in life?
2. Which positive attributes about you do you appreciate most?
3. Where do you feel success with your priorities?

QUESTIONS FOR DIRECTION (GETTIN' BETTER)

1. What parts of life or work do you feel like you need to be more intentional?
2. Which aspects of your purpose need further consideration and thought?
3. How can you improve from the inside out rather than the outside in?

CHAPTER 6

BE ACCOUNTABLE

"People are more inclined to pass the buck than they are to take responsibility. The fact is, though, passing the buck doesn't build your character or give you the opportunity to learn from your mistakes."
— Marshall Goldsmith

When I was a child, the barbershop I went to had a sign that said:

Teenagers: Stop! Move out, get a job, and start a family while you still know everything!

I didn't fully understand that sign then...but I'm starting to grasp it now! I'm not sure I can say the same for society, though. It appears in our "information age," everyone wants to know it all. Answers to almost any question are just a quick Google search or AI prompt away. All the world's knowledge is seemingly at the tips of our fingers. We must not be deceived, however, to think that just because knowledge and facts are so readily available, we are the all-knowing ones. It is one thing to be educated or informed and another thing altogether to be wise and disciplined with what we do with what we know.

That's where the perspective and accountability of others comes in and helps us. To be sure, wisdom is gained by experience, but it doesn't have to be *our* personal experiences. We can take advantage of others' experiences and learn their lessons for ourselves. There is much power in wise counsel.[39] Taking the stories and situations of others and being willing to consider their different points of view helps provide vision to areas that we are unable to see on our own. It can also provide affirmation and attention, which gives positive energy to our hopes and ambitions.

The biggest mistake many leaders make is presuming their worldview is the normal and right one and refusing to acknowledge the legitimacy of other possibilities. That kind of prideful approach is what a friend of mine called stinkin' thinkin'. Often, the reason our results stink is our attitude, which is too prideful to enlist the support of others. As we know, the same old thinking is going to get the same old results. A lot of people don't consider alternate routes, viewpoints, or suggestions for an issue. It's a strange thing that a person would rather be stuck than seek and receive advice from someone else.

Legendary football coach Nick Saban says, "Average players want to be left alone. Good players want to be coached. Great players want to be told the truth."[40] Coach Saban grasped clearly the value of a champion's mindset regarding receiving both the praise and criticism of others. Improvers are winners, too. And that's why we'll spend the next few pages discussing improving ourselves and others through the application of accountability, encouragement, and feedback. We do this so we can be great winners in each of life's domains.

NEVER AGAIN

When I was around twenty years old, I found myself in quite a predicament. My utilities, namely water and electricity, had been disconnected from the mobile home I was renting due to non-payment. The non-payment was not an oversight; I was broke. I had been on a diet of ramen noodles and one-dollar-menu fast food. My spending was not extravagant, and my expenses were low, yet as a student minister at a local church, my income was even lower. (To be clear, the church compensated me fairly, but youth ministry is not a lucrative career.)

I needed money, and I needed it fast. Someone would have to bail me out. I reasoned within myself how embarrassing and awkward it would be to go to my church, which was my employer, to ask for an advance or a financial gift. I knew there was another church in town – by appearance, the biggest and wealthiest one – that might be of service. After all, I knew of other people the church had supported in their times of need. From my angle, I fit the profile of a good, honest person who was just down on my luck and needed a hand.

So, there I am sitting in the office of the mission pastor of a neighboring church requesting financial assistance to help with my bills. Throughout the conversation, the pastor was very thorough in making a proper discovery of what led to my dilemma. And it was his diligence that allowed him to discover the truth.

The truth was that my utilities were disconnected because I hadn't paid my bills. I hadn't paid my bills because I used my paycheck from my church/employer to pay off my payday loan (facepalm). I had a payday loan because the credit card company had scared me into using all my available cash to pay off my balance, which was over the limit. Why would a young college student like me have a maxed-out credit card in the first place? It was the result of a shopping binge I took one day after going through a break-up with my then-girlfriend. The flat-screen TV with surround sound, DVD player, and entertainment stand was therapeutic to my immature soul.

I had not shared the factors of my financial brokeness or my materialistic method of coping with anyone until then, and little did I know I was in for a rude awakening. The pastor began his response by saying, "Justin, what I am about to do is what the Bible has commanded us to do – 'speak truth in love.' You may not agree that it's true, and it may not feel like love, but that's my motivation...Now, brother, first off, you need to realize that it's 'Christians' like you who give other Christians like me a bad name. You have been selfish and immature. You have been lacking wisdom and self-control. God has put you in a place of shepherding others, yet you have not been able to shepherd yourself. You should be in a position of *giving*, but you are attempting to *take* from those in need...Our benevolence fund is here for those who are victims of their circumstances, not the direct cause of them." (Ouch!)

He continued, "Our church will not become an enabler and bail you out of your financial situation, but we will give you a small gift." He reached around behind his desk and pulled one of the several copies of Dave Ramsey's *The Total Money Makeover* off the shelf. He said, "Take this and read it as soon as possible. If you have questions, I'm no financial advisor, but I'll help educate you the best I can on wisdom in your finances." After he said a quick prayer over me, which I was too frustrated and angry to pay attention to, I left his office.

I found my way to my little Chevrolet single-cab pickup. I closed the door, and right in the church parking lot, I wept like I hadn't wept in years. I decided I would never again be in that situation. Never again would I be forced to ask anyone else for money because I had been reckless and foolish with my money. Never again would I be so irresponsible. It was time to grow up. I made a "never again" promise to myself (and to this day have kept it).

I grabbed the book he gave me, read it within a few days, and immediately began implementing practices of budgeting, debt reduction, and generosity. That day changed the entire trajectory of my life. The attitude and behavior shift from that moment has led to experiences and opportunities I never dreamed possible. All because someone else had wisdom – a better perspective – that I didn't have and was willing to share it and hold me accountable. I'm grateful for someone who "spoke truth in love" to my situation. This one step towards a new perspective created a lasting impact and altered my life trajectory. You might be one step away from someone speaking into your circumstances so powerfully that your life could be forever changed.

INCONVENIENT TRUTH

In 2006, LSU was down 3-7 to rival Auburn in a riveting football game. Quarterback Jamarcus Russell dropped back and threw a pass to his receiver at the goal line. In a stadium with almost 90,000 fans, something remarkably interesting happened. All the fans for LSU raised their hands and signaled catch, while all the fans for Auburn waved their hands side-to-side and shouted incomplete.

Everyone observed the same event. However, there were completely different conclusions about what transpired. What caused their perception of reality to contradict? The reason is that the fans came with their preconceived ideas and notions of which team they wanted to win; they already had their side chosen and their champion picked before the game even started. Their bias affected their judgment to the point that what they "saw" with their own eyes might not even be what really happened. (For those curious, it turns out that the pass was dropped due to pass interference – as clearly shown by the replay.)

I think this is the way many of us approach life and business. We've already chosen our sides and staked out our positions stubbornly refusing reasonable consideration of alternatives that would be inconvenient.

French mathematician and physicist Blaise Pascal once said, "People almost invariably arrive at their beliefs not on the basis of proof but on the basis of what they find attractive."[41] The Improver must resist this temptation. We should be reasonable and open to helpful feedback from others.

At the heart, that's what healthy accountability is—helpful feedback. Accountability is a combination of another person's point of view combined with your agreement and expectation to meet a specified standard. This standard could be rules or laws designated by a group of people, a commitment between you and another person, or a personal goal you have set for yourself. In all cases, there's a benchmark or level by which you are measuring success, and when you fail to meet that standard, whoever enforces consequences on you is bringing accountability.

If you are unsure whether or not you have someone holding you accountable, one indicator is whether or not they bring inconvenient truth to you. To be an Improver, inconvenient truths have to be seen as assets, not threats, that will help us grow healthy, increase our influence, and expand our impact.

INPUT-OUTPUT CYCLE

People desire better results and an improved reality but struggle with how to change their circumstances. No matter how much motivation and hope they can muster, positive change seems to escape them.

Here's the deal—your reality, whether personal or professional, is mostly a consequence of your habits and processes. And your habits and processes are simply a culmination of your actions and behaviors, which are primarily influenced by your attitudes and beliefs. Your attitudes and beliefs are shaped by a combination of the culture around you and the thoughts you entertain. If you want to change your reality, it starts with changing the thoughts you think—those stories you tell yourself—sometimes without even realizing it.

Jon Acuff calls those stories "soundtracks" that we allow to play in the background.[42] The real secret of improvement, growth, and success is mastering our mental playlist and the internal stories we tell ourselves. This order of mental thoughts shaping our circumstances is visualized through the *Input-Output Cycle*.

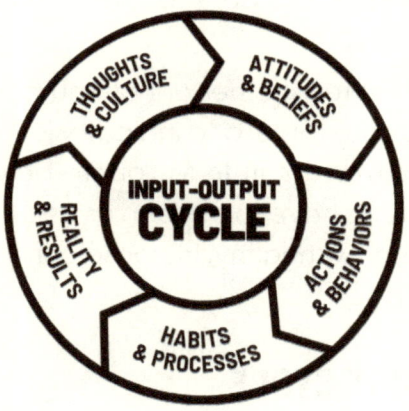

Realizing your reality and results over time can be changed by adjusting what you allow to inform and influence you is empowering. What you're really doing is shaping your inner voice. You're combating the limiting beliefs and false ideas that have held you back. When your internal narrative changes and gets better, it seems like everything changes and gets better.

Jesus refers to this concept in Matthew 6:22 where he says, "The eye is the lamp of the body. If your eye is healthy, your whole body will be full of light."[43] What he is getting at here is that the nature of information and content you allow to enter your mind will bear itself out in your reality. The quality level of what you choose to perceive in your surroundings will have a significant effect on how you will act as a result. What goes in influences what comes out.

Without a doubt, the fastest and most effective way to rewrite the counter-productive messages you tell yourself is to build your inner circle and let them speak into your life. A lot of your thoughts and attitudes are shaped by those you spend the most time with. Your inner voice is created in large part by your inner circle. Change your circle, change your life.

NO B.S.

It's a little cliché, but I wouldn't be where I am today if it weren't for my inner circle. Of course, this includes my family and business associates, however, I'm thinking of a different type of inner circle. Some close friends of mine and I decided to get together for a weekly breakfast when I was in the early stages of entrepreneurship. The group was formed initially just for casual conversation and connection, but over time developed into a strong fellowship.

Now, I need to stop right here because some people, when they read the word fellowship, think of potluck dinners in the church dining area or a higher education development program. That's not what I mean here. Think more like *Lord of the Rings: Fellowship of the Ring*[44]. That fictional version of fellowship was about a bunch of different races (elves, dwarves, men, hobbits, etc.) traversing tumultuous landscapes, facing terrifying evil, and overcoming all odds to achieve victory. That's the kind of fellowship God has in mind for us; one with a noble mission where we are stronger together in our diversity and support one another for the journey. That kind of fellowship I'm referring to here.

One of the practices we had in our fellowship group was "No B.S. Talks." No B.S. was a double entendre, with the first meaning being what you typically think of when you hear "B.S.," which is "no bull-&#%!." The other meaning was no *blind spots*. When one of us guys would approach another and say, "I need to have a *No B.S. Talk* with you," it translated, "I'm going to be very honest with you, I'm not holding back, and I'm assuming the thing I'm bringing up is something you're unaware of and doing unintentionally (i.e., a blind spot)." When you were approached for a No B.S. Talk, you knew you were about to have something pointed out about you that's probably not flattering.

An example of this could be something like, "Hey, Justin. I need to have a No B.S. talk with you." I acknowledge, take a breath, and brace myself. "In our conversations, I don't think you mean to do this, but you interrupt when others are speaking. Sometimes we feel disrespected and like you're trying to hog the attention. I don't think that's your intention, so wanted to let you know."

→ *Consider this:* Do you see the power in a conversation like this? Would having these types of relationships and "talks" be meaningful and beneficial for you?

What a gift these conversations were. To have someone who cares about you speak truth in love and point out an area where you lack self-awareness is the equivalent of having a wingman in an aircraft formation. It's someone who "has your six" and is there to keep you safe and on point. You have more vision and more strength as a result.

Your inner circle of accountability partners should include people who will tell you:

— No.
— Are you sure?
— Have you thought about it this way?
— That was inappropriate.

Remember Ian Cron? He's the expert on the Enneagram personality typing and self-awareness system mentioned in the first chapter. One of the questions he encourages people to ask others is, "What do you know about me that I apparently don't know about me, but I should?"[45] That question is proactively soliciting a challenging *No B.S. Talk* to eliminate blind spots and increase self-awareness.

Of course, you had better make sure that whomever you offer this question is someone you can be vulnerable with and has your best interest at heart; otherwise, you might open yourself up to some overly critical and unhelpful feedback. Or, on the other end of the spectrum, flattery, which is just as dangerous. You should only ask for No B.S. Talks from someone with the heart of a teacher who will care and correct in balance.

My best friend, Adam, is a fantastic example of employing these accountability principles. I always let him know any time I have to travel out of town or stay overnight by myself since traveling alone, particularly on overnight trips, is a point of strong temptation and a high-risk environment for many people. We've all heard the stories, and I didn't want to become one, so I enlisted Adam as an accountability partner. He can call or text any time while I'm traveling to get a status check, and he's done that many times. That simple possibility of a call or follow-up question when I return provides a level of accountability that supports my desire to stay faithful. Everyone needs people like this in their inner circle.

The inner circle of the Improver consists of those who applaud and affirm your successes while helping you rebound and learn from your failures. They will challenge you to a higher standard as they cheer you forward towards the goal.

One other note here is that a healthy inner circle is not always about helping you figure out exactly *what to do* as much as it is about reminding you of *who you are*. When we get discouraged or distracted, we can lose sight of our true selves. Stress and fear can prompt us to act in ways outside of our genuine character. When our fellowship consists of people who are fighting for our good and keep us centered, we can make progress in what we need to do and what we need to be.

COMPASSIONATE CURIOSITY

There is a Diminisher approach to accountability, which makes people and situations worse, and an Improver approach, which makes people and situations better. (Existers aren't included here because they don't exert energy for accountability; they deflect, ignore, or abdicate issues.)

The Improver type of accountability is positive, future-oriented, and uplifting. The Diminisher type is negative, blame-oriented, and discouraging. See the comparisons below:

DIMINISHER *vs* IMPROVER
ACCOUNTABILITY ACCOUNTABILITY

DIMINISHER	IMPROVER
focuses on the past	focuses on the future
creates defensiveness	creates openness
calls a person out	calls a person up
questions the value of the player	questions the validity of the play
fuels team division and conflict	fuels team unity and learning
results in resentment and failure	results in learning and growth

The secret ingredient of Improver Accountability is *compassionate curiosity*. Compassionate curiosity looks for ways to serve the other person and lift them up. Compassionate curiosity presumes good intentions and is genuinely interested in understanding all perspectives in a situation. Those who are compassionately curious know the power of calm, open-ended questions and avoiding harsh criticisms or accusations. For the Improver who aims to be accountable, you do not want to be a victim of a Diminisher accountability, so accept into your inner circle only those who are marked by a spirit of compassionate curiosity.

Once you have a person or people who are employing Improver Accountability for you, being willing and able to receive and accept what they bring is vital. If your circle gives you feedback and you consistently disregard it, they'll stop wasting their time. Musician Frank Zappa said, "A mind is like a parachute, it doesn't work if it's not open." If you have an open mind and an open heart, putting together an inner circle that has your back and holds you accountable is incredibly powerful. As an Improver, you'll limit growth and progress with a lone wolf approach, but your ability to give and receive accountability and feedback is paramount to mission success.

In many ways, going through life and business is like a maze. We have a vague idea of the start and finish, but there are a lot of twists, turns, and dead ends along the way. Often, our apparent progress is thwarted by a surprising barrier or dead end that leads us to retrace steps and feel like we're going in circles, which can be incredibly frustrating and discouraging. What would make finding our way out of a maze much easier would be having a source, like a drone, to share directions with us. Since we don't have that type of drone for life's maze, we need others to speak into our situations and hold us accountable. We need them to help with our B.S. and offer their compassionate curiosity as they support and challenge us. Having feedback from a trusted frienc, mentor, or coach who has a distinct perspective, resources, and experiences is invaluable and a requirement fcr the Improver to fulfill his or her potential and purpose.

KEY POINTS

1. To the degree we limit feedback and the perspective of others, we limit our growth and our impact.
2. Accountability includes speaking truth in love to those you are in fellowship with.
3. We need others in our inner circle to help us with strength and vision.

QUESTIONS FOR REFLECTION (GOOD)

1. When did someone hold you accountable in a healthy way?
2. Who had your back during a tough time in your life or business?
3. Where do you feel like you have been open-minded and growing lately?

QUESTIONS FOR DIRECTION (GETTIN' BETTER)

1. What areas might you need accountability so you can improve?
2. In what ways could your inner circle be strengthened?
3. How healthy is the culture of accountability for your team?

CHAPTER 7:

SERVE OTHERS

"Don't look for big things,
just do small things with great love."
— Mother Teresa

In 2019, NBA Hall of Famer Kareem Abdul-Jabbar made headlines by selling his four championship rings, three MVP trophies, and other memorabilia for $2.8 million. The proceeds were dedicated to a youth education program. Reflecting on his decision, Abdul-Jabbar said, "When it comes to choosing between storing a championship ring or trophy in a room or providing kids with an opportunity to change their lives, the choice is pretty simple: Sell it all."

Kareem gets it. He knows what it means to be a person of significance and impact, prioritizing what matters most. Living a life of service and generosity is what brings true joy, peace, and happiness to our lives. And that's why the fifth step of the *Daily High Five*, to serve others, matters so much—it's what brings meaning and fulfillment to the world.

It reminds me of a teacher who brought balloons to school and asked his students to blow them all up and then had them all write their names on one of the balloons. Once they wrote their names on the balloons they tossed them in the hallway while the teacher mixed them from one end to the other.

The teacher then gave them five minutes to find the balloon with their name on it. The students ran around looking frantically but as time ran out, nobody had found their own balloon. Then the teacher told them to take the balloon closest to them and give it to the person whose name was on it. In less than two minutes, everyone had their balloon.

Finally, the teacher said "Balloons are like happiness. No one will find it looking for only their own balloon. Instead, if everyone cares about each other they will help one another find theirs as quickly as possible so everyone wins."

In middle school, I was taught that high self-esteem was a characteristic of utmost value. However, Philippians 2:3-4 says that we should "esteem others" as more important than ourselves. And to "look out not only for his own interests, **but also for the interests of others.**"[46] Instead of being inwardly focused, being others-focused is the way to go.

Zig Ziglar's most famous quote is, "You can have everything in life you want if you will just help other people get what they want."[47] This chapter is about how your life can be more significant, meaningful and enjoyable as you help, serve, and give to others.

HATS OF SERVICE

One of my all-time favorite movie scenes is from Darkest Hour, which features Gary Oldman as Winston Churchill. The setting is early in the days of World War II, and Churchill is preparing to give a speech to the House of Commons. He and his wife, Clemmie, are having a brilliant conversation as she tries to offer encouragement for the momentous day.

She tries to inspire him by saying, "Go, be... be yourself."

Churchill in his witty manner of speaking responds, "Which self?"

The moment is vividly accentuated as he turns to a wall on which many hats are hung—club caps, Admiral's hats, top hats, riding hats, and more. As he contemplates his choice of hat for the day, he is also seemingly envisioning what type of presence and image he intends to display as he goes through his endeavors. The variety of hat color and style options is as diverse as his personality.

While "be yourself" might feel like appropriate advice regardless of the situation, the truth is the way we share our "self" with others may look quite different from day to day. When it comes to serving people, there are endless options as diverse as our personalities and various areas of giftedness. Which option we choose for the benefit others can vary based on our situation and season of life. Yet, as Winston had his preferred go-to hats, there are a few hats that we can wear daily to help others. There are five primary roles that are available to all of us as we serve people:

1. **Collaborative Partner**
2. **Meaningful Mentor**
3. **Insightful Advisor**
4. **Dedicated Friend**
5. **Joyous Giver**

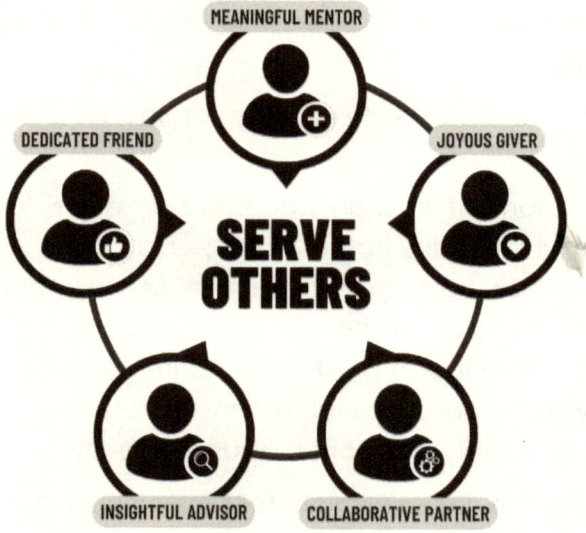

COLLABORATIVE PARTNER

One way we serve others is by partnering with them. This doesn't necessarily mean a business partnership, although that is a possibility. When we speak of being a partner here, we are saying that we are becoming teammates with someone. You collaborate with them and participate in helping them achieve desired results.

This is where the principle of synergy comes into play: just as two horses can pull more together than the sum of what they can pull individually, partnering with someone helps them accomplish more with less effort. John Lennon and Paul McCartney of The Beatles are a classic example of a collaborative partnership. Their joint songwriting efforts produced some of the most iconic songs in music history. By blending their unique talents and creative processes, they created music that has endured for generations.

For an example involving more team members, do an online video search for "FORMULA 1 racing pit crews." It's amazing to see more than twenty people change tires and make adjustments to the race car in less than three seconds.

When you serve others by being a collaborative partner, you roll up your sleeves, work together on goals, and build alongside one another, creating results that surpass individual capabilities.

→ *Consider this:* Who can you team up with to achieve a shared goal? How can you be a better collaborator?

MEANINGFUL MENTOR

Becoming a meaningful mentor is another option for creating exponential impact in the life of another person. While a partner helps you focus on your results, a mentor focuses on your development. Mentors are typically more inclined to focus on personal growth and development over career advancement or professional ambitions. Consider a senior employee who takes a new hire under their wing, offering guidance not just on job tasks but also on navigating office culture and career growth. Or a biblical example would be the Apostle Paul who tenderly but firmly helps young Timothy to gain his footing in the faith and ministry.

If you help someone by becoming a meaningful mentor, you're an unofficial counselor to help that individual become and remain healthy. Not only is this a way to help others, but mentoring allows you to see the growth and success of those you guide, which can be incredibly rewarding and validating.

→ *Consider this:* Who in your life could benefit from your guidance? What steps can you take to become a more effective mentor?

INSIGHTFUL ADVISOR

Insightful advisors are meticulous and dialed in on facts. If you become an advisor to someone, you are helping them by bringing knowledge, expertise, and truth to the situation. Your gift to them is clarity and understanding. While a mentor is more like a counselor, advisors are more akin to consultants. The former leans a little more towards the heart, while the latter leans more towards the head.

An insightful advisor is a lighthouse, guiding ships through the fog with clear and unwavering signals. They bring clarity and direction to the desired destination. The obvious examples here include professionals like financial advisors, attorneys, and my personal favorite, executive coaches.

One condition here is to remember uninformed opinions are not the same as qualified advice. In your efforts to help someone, you can cause harm by offering bad counsel. If you desire to wear this advisor hat, you should be knowledgeable, and when applicable, certified or credentialed. That said, so long as you are operating in truth and a desire to build up, helping someone logically navigate a situation is an incredibly significant way to serve others.

→ *Consider this:* What areas of expertise can you share with others? How can you ensure your advice is well-informed and beneficial?

DEDICATED FRIEND

Although we might not intuitively think of it, a wonderful way of serving people is being a dedicated friend. Dedicated friends focus on their relationship with a person and supporting that individual's well-being. Think of a someone who checks in regularly, offers a listening ear during tough times, and celebrates your successes as if they were their own. A dedicated friend is a sturdy oak tree, providing shade and shelter through all seasons of life.

J.R.R. Tolkien and C.S. Lewis shared a deep and dedicated friendship. They supported each other's writing careers and personal lives, meeting regularly to discuss their works and offer mutual encouragement. Their friendship was a source of strength and inspiration, demonstrating the profound impact a dedicated friend can have.

The depth of your friendship is directly correlated with how much you care about the person. You know the people that feed your soul, because you feel good after spending time with them. My wife, Kathryn, and I have a core friends group that we refer to as our "framily," because they are friends that have become like family. Having experienced the first couple of years of our marriage without deep, long-lasting connections, I can attest the power of having committed friends come alongside and do life together with you.

If you are a dedicated friend to someone else, they'll feel uplifted after being with you, and they know you are committed to them. People sense the difference when they have someone who prays for them, encourages them, and is there to support them in the highs and lows. When someone is treated like that, they sense they are valued and included - what an amazing way to serve!

→ *Consider this:* How can you deepen your friendships? What can you do to show your friends that you are truly dedicated to their well-being?

JOYOUS GIVER

The last of these roles of serving is being a joyous giver. Joyous givers are the fuel that empowers the hopes and goals of others. The most natural way of doing this is by offering financial support, but if you are a joyous giver, you will also sacrifice your time, talents, energy, and other physical resources. Generous givers are hospitable and willing to volunteer to help others.

While many celebrities, professional athletes, and politicians support charitable causes from afar, certain individuals like Tim Tebow are known for giving more than just their dollars. Tebow is known for his philanthropic efforts through the Tim Tebow Foundation, which focuses on various initiatives, including providing care for children with special needs, building hospitals, and supporting adoption services. Tebow's Night to Shine events, which are prom nights for people with special needs, exemplify his joyous giving spirit. He is often present and participating in these events—truly the heart of an Improver!

Being a joyous giver is a win-win, because not only does sharing generously make a smoother path for others through kindness and generosity, it can bring a sense of purpose and happiness, as you see the positive impact of your gifts on others' lives. Perhaps contributing a meal to a family in need, volunteering for an improvement project, surprising an acquaintance with a gift, or hosting a neighbor in your home is your next action step to be a blessing and serve others as an Improver.

→ *Consider this:* What resources or talents can you share with others? How can you give more joyfully and generously?

These five roles represent significant ways you can help others. People need our perspective, our presence, and our prayers. They need us to show up with positive energy and help. They need our ideas. We have diverse personalities, talents, and giftedness that should be used to build up others. By taking advantage of opportunities to do life and business together, we create more productivity, support, comfort, connection, and protection for people. This truly makes the world a better place.

OTP & 3L'S

In high school and early college, I took people's grace and patience for granted. I was naïve to the way I treated others regarding their time. One of my meaningful mentors finally brought this to my attention. He had invited me over to his home weekly, where he would provide breakfast and encouragement. I was young in ministry, and he had spent more than 50 years in those circles. He had a lot of wisdom to share. The problem was I would often oversleep and show up late. When I did arrive, many times I would become distracted and begin thinking about various people and situations, not paying full attention to the wisdom this man was so generously offering.

One morning, he'd had enough. "Justin, you aren't really taking this seriously, are you? You call yourself a Christian, but Jesus said, 'Let your yes be yes and your no be no.'" He went on to say, "If you want me to continue opening my home and meeting with you, I will, but this is your last chance. You'd better be on time and present."

That last phrase was loud and clear, so I wrote in my planner, "OTP for Mentor Breakfast." OTP is short for "on time and present." For the past twenty years, I've been using that descriptor for most of my appointments. It serves as my reminder to not just show up but show up on time (which means early) and be fully present. It's amazing to me how many "professionals" consistently arrive late for important appointments and then allow themselves to be interrupted by their smartphones during the time allotted to meet.

Some of my friends refer to these people as "marsh-mallows" because their word is soft and squishy, whereas an Improver's agreement to be somewhere or do some-thing is a firm commitment. One of the most practical ways to serve people is to respect them by showing up on time for meetings and being present.

Our business was growing, and it was time to add members to the team, so we sponsored a booth at a local job fair with the hopes of attracting several qualified ap-plicants at once. In the days preceding the event, I was excited about meeting candidates in person and having the opportunity to get to know them face-to-face.

The day before the event, I was making my big three to-dos for the next day and wrote: *OTP for the Job Fair*. Not long after jotting that down, I was reminded of the Dale Carnegie principle: "The most *interesting* person in the room is the most *interested* person in the room."[48] I became convicted about my mental approach to the job fair. I had been imagining all the ways that more good people on my team would make my life and busi-ness better, the problems they would solve for me, and the growth they would bring to me. Up to this point, all my thoughts about the event were about me: my hopes, my dreams, and my ambitions; I wasn't truly interested in them.

I started to imagine the situation these applicants were in. Some had recently been laid off. Others were trying to get their first job out of college. Several had been forced to relocate from other regions and needed work. Virtually all the prospective employees were anxious about their future. This fair was an opportunity for them to drastically improve their circumstances and positively alter their life trajectory. On the way to the venue, my wife and I discussed what these candidates truly needed and how we might serve them well. Three words surfaced from our conversation:

1. **Listen** – From a practical standpoint, we would learn far more about the applicant by listening instead of talking. From a moral standpoint, this was a way to honor and serve them.

2. **Learn**—Being curious and compassionate about their story, discovering their true strengths and personalities, and understanding their aspirations was beneficial for them and us.

3. **Love**—We committed to making sure each applicant who came by our booth felt encouraged, appreciated, and loved. We would do our best to inspire and equip them in their journey.

I went back to my to-do list and added "3Ls" to my task list so that it read: *OTP & 3Ls for Job Fair*. I now format almost every important appointment that way. When I meet with people, I strive to show up on time and be fully present as I listen, learn, and love. I'm not perfect in this endeavor, and sometimes, my ego gets in the way of listening well, but this framework has helped me help others.

Oh, and we didn't get any rockstar employees from that event, however, we walked away feeling like a million bucks. It was the right way to treat people, and it's always the right thing to treat people the right way.

A LASTING LEGACY

Memento mori is a Latin term that means "remember you will die." It's a call to recognize life's brevity and death s certainty, urging us to value each moment. Traditionally depicted with skulls, bones, coffins, and clocks, this concept oozes a certain cool, edgy vibe. In real life, however, it's more complex to embody this idea because, most of the time, we don't feel like we will die.

Comprehending our own mortality is tough, as death feels both distant and abstract, expected to happen far in the future. I mentioned earlier in the book that in my early twenties, I discovered I had cancer. As a child, I had multiple living grandparents and great-grandparents, and I even knew my great-great-grandmother. I had always imagined growing old like them, but the reality of death was staring me in the face as a young college student, and it was sobering.

When most people consider that life is like a vapor, here for a brief time and then vanishes away (James 4:14), they think of their legacy. How will they be remembered? How will people speak of them when they are gone? Did their life matter?

Legacy may sound a lot like impact, and it is, but in my view, there is a nuanced difference between legacy and impact. The distinction is one of measure. An impact can be infrequent and small. On the other hand, legacy is impact repeatedly multiplied and magnified. When an incredible legacy is created, it is always due to a series of consistent, meaningful impacts. A person with habits of inspiring the lives of those he or she meets leads to exponential impact, which is another way of saying, a lasting legacy.

How does one go about creating a meaningful legacy? In short, the answer is serving others. The greatest returns on investments you will ever make are in the lives of those you touch.

My friend, Kyle Gabhart, is the founder and owner of Bluegrass Legacy Group. He writes in his book, *Legends Don't Retire*:

> "When we think of legacy, we often think of something left behind. While this is true, real legends live their legacy each day, one day at a time, allowing them the opportunity to experience the value they are creating and be a part of the impact they are making...By shifting our perspective from leaving a legacy to living a legacy, we seize the opportunity to take an active role in the story we tell."[49]

You shape your legacy by your actions. How you approach conversations, your work, and events is either making deposits or withdrawals into the life accounts of others. If you desire to be an Improver, your pattern will be one of deposits more than withdrawals. Improvers wear those hats of being a giver, advisor, partner, friend, and mentor.

I once heard it said that how many times you hear the word *thanks* or *thank you* is a measuring stick for the amount of meaning in your life. What if your legacy was not defined by sales transactions or points scored but by the number of people feeling and expressing a heart-felt gratitude for how you added value to them? Improvers should hear "thanks" and "thank you" multiple times a day because we should be focused on serving others.

UNLEASH GREATNESS

There is no greater example of serving people than Jesus Christ, and He has the ultimate legacy. He came and lived a life defined by lifting others up, speaking truth to their circumstances, and providing opportunities for transformation. He perfectly emulated all five roles of service: advising on truth, mentoring on how to live, partnering in mission, being a friend, and a joyful giver to the highest degree. No one on this planet has come close to Jesus's influence and impact. He says about himself in Matthew 20:28, "…[I] did not come to be served, but to serve…"[50] This was his heartbeat, and it should be ours.

Building our legacy should be motivated by helping others. Our legacy only matters as far as it points people in the right direction and encourages them on the path of love, peace, and truth. The Matthew passage above was in response to Jesus' disciples arguing over who would get the places of honor and authority in the coming kingdom. Jesus reminded them what it meant to be genuinely great, and that is sacrificing for others.

In 2023, we hosted an Improver leadership conference themed "Unleash Greatness." The purpose of the event was to empower leaders with everything they need to create a thriving legacy and unleash a positive and powerful impact on their circles of influence. We brought in top-notch speakers from around the country and the message that continued to surface was one of meeting the needs of others.

Kyle Draper, motivational speaker and founder of Hire Culture VA, said in one of the keynotes, "I care more about helping people than looking stupid. I care more about serving people than appearing to be more successful than I am." Kyle consistently encourages his followers on social media to put the ego aside and help people. Amen, brother.

Truly unleashing greatness is not about increasing your societal standing and reputation or even building a positive legacy for yourself; it's about making a real difference in people's lives. Diminishers and Existers prioritize their pride, comfort, and appetite, but Improvers sacrifice these things.

To be the person you are meant to be, you must change your paradigm from being about you to being about others. Lay aside ego and put on one of the hats of service by giving, partnering, advising, mentoring, or just being a friend. The world needs Improvers ready, willing, and able to serve others now more than ever. I hope you'll join us.

KEY POINTS

1. Serving others and being generous leads to joy, meaning, and fulfillment in life.
2. Opportunities are presented daily for us to wear different roles (or "hats") of service such as being a collaborative partner, meaningful mentor, insightful advisor, dedicated friend, or joyous giver.
3. The legacy of greatness that we create is directly proportional to how we impact others.

QUESTIONS FOR REFLECTION (GOOD)

1. What "hat of service" have you worn lately: collaborative partner, meaningful mentor, insightful advisor, dedicated friend, or joyous giver?
2. Who has left (or is leaving) a lasting legacy in your life, and what qualities and actions do they display?
3. What do you feel are the positive aspects of your legacy?

QUESTIONS FOR DIRECTION (GETTIN' BETTER)

1. In what ways can you expand your roles as a service-oriented individual, such as becoming a more collaborative partner, a more insightful advisor, or a more joyous giver?
2. What changes can you make to be punctual, present, and purposeful (OTP & 3Ls) in your meetings with others?
3. Which areas of your life might success, pride, ego, or comfort be keeping you from unleashing greatness?

CHAPTER 8

HOW HIGH IS UP?

"The primary ingredient for progress is optimism. The unwavering belief that something can be better is what drives the human race forward."
— *Simon Sinek*

I'm thankful for this phrase: "You've got potential." Growing up, it's one of the messages that was repeated to me. Grandparents, neighbors, teachers at school, people at church, and more would comment, "he's got great potential." Others looked at me and would remark, "he's going places."

What a privilege to have that kind of blessing spoken to you over many years by so many people. Do you know what happened over time? I started to think these people were right. I began to trust that I had a good future ahead and that the best was yet to come. I believed in my potential then, and still do now. It's one of the things that makes me an Improver – intentionally trying to fulfill potential.

Later in life, as I delved into the business world, I heard a co-worker state, "We're asking ourselves 'how high is up?'" It was a peculiar way of saying, "We think there is a lot of potential here and we want to maximize that and go as high and far as we can as a team." I'm sure you've had similar thoughts and feelings personally and professionally as well.

One of the big questions of life we tend to ask ourselves as we mature is on the topic of potential. Specifically, that internal wondering that we reflect on from time to time: What is my true ability? What can I *really* do for the world? How big of an impact can I make? The answers to these questions can influence our life journey significantly, which is why this chapter is so important.

I see this vividly in the interaction of kids with one another, especially boys. Have you ever watched a game of "King of the Hill" or "Red Rover" ...or any kind of play with young boys? Everything, and I mean everything, turns into a competition. But I don't think their nature is only about seeing where they rank among their peers and who the alpha of the group is. I believe it's also about testing their limits to see how far *they* can go individually. Even unknowingly, they want to know their potential.

What's true of kids on the playground is true of us adults in the real world; we question our potential and strive to test our limits. As Improvers, we are incredibly inspired by understanding our capacity and become very excited when we feel like we are maximizing our potential.

POTENTIAL IS POWERFUL

Word studies are sometimes overused, but there is a lot of meaning in the definition and etymology for potential. Merriam-Webster states that potential is "existing in possibility; something that can develop or become actual." Potential exists in possibility, not in reality. Sounds vague and philosophical to me. You too? Let's explore further.

Potential is derived from the Latin *potentialis* or *potentia*, meaning 'power'. Similarly, *potentia* is from the Greek word *dunamis*, which is where we get the word dynamite. Dynamite! Now we're getting somewhere. The idea of potential is like a stick of dynamite – it is powerful, and its impact is incredible. Until the fuse is lit, however, it's just something "existing in possibility" that "can develop" or "could happen (but hasn't)."

You may already know where this is going. Potential is that which has power or potency that *can be* but *has not yet* come into existence or sight. It is unexposed capability, reserved power, untapped strengths, hidden talents, and dormant gifts. As it relates to you and me, potential is the ability and possibility to do and become more. It's realizing increased power and making a bigger impact.

With that in mind, think through the list above again:

— dormant ability
— untapped strength
— unused success
— hidden talents
— capped capability

Which of these makes you notice unrealized potential in your own life? When you review that list and think about those people you love and lead, where do you think you can more effectively provide support and challenge?

On the other end of the scale is actuality, which is potentiality that has been fulfilled, made real, or brought into being. While many (most?) people may be saddened or frustrated by not reaching their potential, for the Improver, it often feels like an absolute tragedy. Missed potential eats at our spirit.

We have an internal drive, an insatiable hunger to fulfill our potential, realize our possibilities, and help others do the same. The problem is that there are typically gaps between what we desire and the outcomes we actually experience, and we aren't sure why our reality doesn't live up to our expectations. For the Improver to realize our potential, we must identify the reasons for this gap in expectations and overcome the barriers holding us back.

BREAKTHROUGH THE BARRIERS

My dad has worked most of his life on rigs drilling for oil and gas. I used to be amazed (actually, I still am!) when he would go out to the Gulf of Mexico or the middle of an east Texas field and drill thousands of feet underground to tap the so-called "black gold." Drilling for oil is a fitting metaphor as we talk about unrealized gains and benefits not yet realized. Just as the vast reserves of oil and gas lay trapped beneath layers of earth and clay, waiting to be discovered and utilized, our true potential often remains buried under the surface of our everyday lives.

Think about it. You have a treasure of hopes, visions, and dreams that are out of reach. There are layers of discouragement, procrastination, failure, opinions, distractions, traditions, and compromise that are keeping you from accessing your most valuable resources. If you want to tap the immense value of all that is within, you must drill through these barriers, carefully navigating to the source.

This is easier said than done. Drilling for oil and gas is a meticulous and determined process. It requires the right tools, expertise, and persistence. The drill must pierce through the hard layers, overcoming challenges to reach the valuable resources below. Similarly, in our personal development, as we strive to tap into our potential, we need the right tools and resources in addition to the proper mindset, knowledge, and determination to push past the barriers that hold us back.

One last application of this metaphor: the moment the drill reaches the oil or gas, it's a breakthrough, unleashing a flow of energy and resources. In our lives, when we finally break through our barriers, we unlock a flow of personal growth, talent, and opportunities. We tap into a reservoir of potential that was always there, waiting to be discovered and utilized.

MENTAL PRISONS

Often, the biggest wall between the life we have and the life we desire is the wall of limiting beliefs we have about ourselves. We hold things to be true about who we are and what we're truly capable of that are not true. Everyone who's not a narcissist has an inner critic that chimes in from time to time, reminding us of our fears and failures, but here's the thing about Improvers – our inner critic is even louder and more degrading than normal. The mental battle that goes on in many of our Improver minds is full of negative self-images and demeaning self-assessments. We reject compliments, devalue our goods and services, and withhold from public view parts of our authentic selves because we've convinced ourselves the world couldn't possibly appreciate and be attracted to the real us.

→ *Consider this:* What part of the "real you" might you be hiding from others? Is it possible that you might be listening too much to your inner critic?

All unfounded beliefs are like prisons. They keep us from going out and reaching our goals. They restrict our ability to imagine and put creativity into action. To take our first steps towards maximizing our potential, we must get out of our self-imposed prisons. Yes, the bad news is we believe false ideas that hold us captive. The good news is we can choose at any time to reject those beliefs and walk in freedom.

Retired cyclist Jamie Paolinetti is one of the most well-known American professional bicycle racers of all time. With over 125 pro victories, he knew how to push himself to victory. He is believed to have said, "Limitations live only in our minds. If we use our imaginations, our possibilities become limitless."

For some of you reading this book, your barrier to potential is a mental limitation you have imposed on yourself. You need only to remind yourself of all that you can become and accomplish and begin walking in that affirmation. Your potential is limitless. Remember, you can do all things through Christ who strengthens you.[51]

APPLE SEEDS TO APPLE TREES

You may have heard the analogy of the apple seeds. When some people see apple seeds, they only see apple seeds that are in the way of the food itself, considered worthless, and thrown away. When other people see apple seeds, they understand all the potential apples (and apple trees) that can come from that seed. They know whenever it's planted, nourished, and taken care of, there is an outstanding and endless ripple effect.

Do you have a knack for recognizing potential or is this a challenge for you? People who are adept at sensing potential and possibilities tend to be able to perceive not only the good potentials of a given situation but also its risks and possible downsides and flaws. Finding that balance between recognizing risk and then recognizing the greater possibilities is part of the balancing act for the Improver.

In the book of Genesis, Satan's lie to Eve in the garden was, in part, that God was limiting her potential and that she only needed to follow his way instead of God's for a more pleasurable and meaningful life. Satan still uses that lie today, "Do it my way, and you won't limit your potential." (My paraphrase.)

This is a good spot to talk about what reaching "full potential" means. First, let's start with God. Unlike people, God has no potentiality in his nature or being—he is all of who he will ever be—the fullness of his nature is and always has been. He is not lacking and has no deficiencies. I often remark to people when they ask how I am doing that, "I'm good and gettin' better." I'm a work in progress, but not God, He's perfectly complete.

As humans, strictly speaking, we will never reach our "full potential" on this side of heaven. One day, when it is our time, we will be made perfect and become everything God intended. I won't be saying "gettin' better" in heaven because I'll be the best version of myself! Our potential and what we are capable of accomplishing now is only constrained by the limits our God has put in place by his sovereignty. For the Christian to reach his potential on earth means he is faithfully carrying out his mission and fulfilling his purpose. Remember discovering your purpose in chapter five? You have a unique *mission* and *message* - a divine purpose. To accomplish your divine purpose is to reach your "full potential," and that purpose (not perfection) is what Improvers should be striving towards each day.

THEOS

The philosopher Aristotle has a model of rhetoric and persuasion that I think helps us understand how to maximize potential. To oversimplify it, there are three appeals of a speaker (or other influencer): *ethos* which refers to the person's credibility or ethics, *logos* which is the message or logic itself, and *pathos* which is the emotional connection by which the concept is being transmitted. His model is highly effective at helping communicators persuade their audience.[52]

Modern-day author and pastor, Louie Giglio, once shared this model and added another factor to the list – *theos*. Theos, he said, is the "God-factor." Giglio argues that a believer can be the right kind of person, saying the right things, the right way, to the right audience, but if he lacks God's favor and blessing, the message will not have its full effect.[53] I find this sentiment to be encouraging and convicting at the same time.

Although the context of both Aristotle and Giglio is focused on communication, I think the principle also applies to life potential. To reach and maximize your potential you must work on yourself (ethos), the task (logos), your relationships and your connections with others (pathos), in addition to seeking God's favor (theos). Simply stated, for you to reach your potential, you need the "God-factor."

Another pastor, the late Charles Stanley, used to encourage his audience to ask these questions to God as a pathway to uncovering their potential[54]:

— What do You want to do in my life?

— What do You want to do through my life?
— What do You still desire for me to experience?

— What possibilities lie within me?

— What potential lies before me?

— What could I become?

— What did You have in mind when you created me?

— What do You desire for me?

These are incredible questions to aid in understanding and unlocking our potential. As you seek to find the answers, begin taking the steps you already know to take. It's worth taking the time to consider that it's possible, perhaps even likely, that some of the most enjoyable and impactful days of your life have not happened yet. I believe there is more in you than you know, but you need God to help you realize it.

Benjamin Zander (the musical conductor mentioned in the second chapter) spoke encouragement into my life from a stage in 2020 when he enthusiastically proclaimed, "Most of us spend our time with an expectation to live up to instead of possibility to live in to." What an amazing way to view our life! Instead of trying to meet the expectations of others (and ourselves), let us look for possibilities and opportunities as we strive to reach our potential. Improver, you have unlimited capacity for growth, influence, and impact, so be encouraged and empowered to go be more of who you were meant to be.

KEY POINTS

1. To the extent we are not reaching our potential, we have dormant abilities, untapped strength, hidden talents, and unused success.
2. Possibilities and opportunities are greater than we can imagine and are only limited by God's plan.
3. Our potential is maximized and realized when we are walking in God's purpose for our lives.

QUESTIONS FOR REFLECTION (GOOD)

1. Which achievement of yours do you remember exceeding your own expectations?
2. What is one of your strengths or talents you have put to good use?
3. Who encouraged you to believe in your potential or hope for a better future?

QUESTIONS FOR DIRECTION (GETTIN' BETTER)

1. Where do you feel like you still have potential for growth, influence, and impact?
2. What comes to mind when you think of where you need the "God-factor" the most right now?
3. How can you focus on God's calling instead of others' expectations?

CHAPTER 9:
WILLING TO CHANGE

"We immediately become more effective when we decide to change ourselves rather than asking things to change for us."
— Stephen Covey

Robert Herjavec is one of the "sharks" from the hit series *Shark Tank*[55]. I remember sitting in a room with a few dozen other entrepreneurs listening to him share an insightful story. After filming one of their episodes, he discussed what the common thread was between all the sharks.

What made them all so successful? How had their life trajectory improved so drastically? What was that common denominator between them all? If it were possible to reduce the secret to their success to one idea, principle, or characteristic, what would it be?

As they made comparisons amongst themselves, they realized how dissimilar they each were: diverse backgrounds, education, industries, and countries of origin.

They were of different races, genders, and ages. They quickly realized if there was a thread between the whole group, it wasn't based on demographic factors.

They began to propose the key factor(s) for winning in business and life must be based on some type of personality or character distinction. One of the sharks suggested, "It's passion – we're enthusiastic about the products or services that we invest in." Mr. Wonderful, Kevin O'Leary, shot back, "No, I'm not passionate about my companies, I'm just greedy," to which everyone responded with a hearty laugh.

Another proposed, "It's our hard work and hustle that made us who we are." Robert responded something to the effect of, "I don't mind rolling my sleeves up, but it was my desire to avoid sweating and stress that helped me develop automated systems and processes for my companies. I wouldn't credit 'grit' with my success."

Ideas were tossed out and discarded over and over for quite some time. Finally, after much debate and discussion, someone in the group threw out a specific word which led to a break in the chatter. Following a few moments of contemplation, the sharks looked around at one another and began to smile and nod. They agreed that this attribute was the X-factor that made them who they were as entrepreneurs more than anything else. The word was *adaptability*.

To them, and anyone else who has been consistently successful in business (or life in general), the ability to quickly respond to market changes and trends, be flexible with shifts and disruptions, and adjust operations, habits, and behaviors to fit the need is the foundation for winning. As the boxers say, "You gotta roll with the punches." That's what many successful people credit with their business success, and it's what's required to be an overcomer in other areas of life as well.

If you put an adaptable person in any environment, their instinct is not to whine or make excuses or pass blame. The natural response of someone truly driven to succeed will be to evaluate their circumstance, consider the options, and take action towards a positive outcome. Change for the sake of change doesn't have any value, but change for the sake of improvement is a price a healthy Improver will gladly pay. As Brian Tracy says, "The future belongs to the competent. Get good, get better, be the best."[56]

Improvers that adapt don't fear the future and they don't fret over change. The classic book, *Who Moved My Cheese?* is an amusing reminder of this principle. You can "Hem and Haw" as you overthink and give way to perfectionist tendencies, or you can "Sniff and Scurry" by stepping into action and following your instincts to new opportunities.[57] But change is difficult and uncomfortable, so we'll spend this chapter getting informed and motivated for positive change.

STANLEY CUPS

One of the most current examples of following the moved cheese is that of the Stanley brand of drinkware. Founded in 1913 by William Stanley, Jr., the company invented the all-steel vacuum bottle, providing customers with a durable, portable, and effective beverage container. William Stanley's death a few years after the launch did not dissuade the company from continuing to innovate and expand its product line, eventually creating a variety of jugs, beverage servers, and decanters.[58]

In 2016, they introduced the 40-ounce Quencher bottle which soon thereafter catapulted Stanley to incredible new heights. Fueled by unexpected viral attention on social media platforms like TikTok, positive exposure to the product increased exponentially. Observing a massive surge in sales, the company scrambled to ramp up its production capacity, however, demand outpaced supply. The item was sold out nationwide, which only increased its appeal due to the principle of exclusivity.

This is where Stanley began to shine as they invested in modern technology, expanded facilities, and formed new partnerships to serve their growing market. They pivoted their marketing strategies to reach their online audience and optimized their distribution channels to get their products into the hands of retailers and consumers. Riding the wave of momentum, they expanded the product line to include new colors, sizes, and features to meet the needs and preferences of their audience.

The agility and responsiveness of Stanley were rewarded as their annual sales skyrocketed from $70 million in 2019 to $750 million in 2023[59]. The growth of the company and brand was initialized by innovating a new product and maximized by adapting to consumer needs in a shifting landscape. While their story is remarkable, it's not a miracle. People reach new heights and achieve higher levels of success than they dreamed possible every day by staying creative, innovative, and adaptive, and you can likewise be better personally and professionally if you are willing to choose that mindset.

LIZARDS, BULLFROGS, AND A GOOSE

David Redding is the founder of an incredible network of peer-led workouts for men called F3. The F3 organization began in 2011 and just 13 years later already has 4,500 workout locations in 365 regions around the world. His perspective on the topic of building effective organizations, which he says are built through relationships, not rules, is particularly creative.

The metaphor he uses is a lizard and bullfrog. The lizard organization is represented as light, fast, and always moving or ready to move. The lizard operates with minimal rules, a specific narrow purpose, and flexibility. Conversely, the bullfrog is bloated, slow, and resistant to change. It adheres to the status quo and is hesitant to expend energy other than to react to its environment as required. The bullfrog is driven primarily by continuity alone (just existing), whereas the lizard proactively moves to find an advantage.[60]

The obvious implication of this analogy is we should aspire to be lizard people and run lizard organizations and reject the way of the bullfrog. This is not at all dissimilar from the way we view being an Exister and an Improver. Bullfrogs are Existers, and Improvers are lizards.

A practical example of this happened at a stage in my career when I was working as an insurance agent at State Farm. State Farm is the largest property and casualty insurance provider in the United States, which offered many impressive advantages of being employed (and insured) with them. One disadvantage, however, was their inherent resistance and slowness to change. In my view, they were, and possibly still are, a bullfrog organization. One of my frustrations working with State Farm was their reliance on fax machines and outdated MS-DOS systems from the 80s to complete basic job functions.

Enter Goosehead Insurance, founded in 2003 (about 80 years after State Farm). The leadership at Goosehead lists as one of their core values, *Relentless Innovation*, which they explain as follows:

> "Not only do we not settle for the status quo; we ignore it completely. We're always thinking bigger and finding new ways to improve our clients and partners' experience."

When I opened my agency there, we were virtually paperless, utilizing e-signature methods and HTML-based sites and programs. The systems were more attractive and intuitive. It's no surprise that Goosehead experienced incredible growth among agencies in regions where their competitors were losing significant market share. Certainly, both Goosehead and State Farm have their competitive pros and cons, but over the long haul, if Goosehead retains its relentless lizard-like mentality, it will likely outpace its good neighbor in the same way Apple outmaneuvered Nokia through consistent innovation.

HAND IN HAND

There is no separating change and growth. Things that grow, change; it's just the way it is. Show me a business or organization that isn't changing, and I'll show you one that is experiencing stagnation and degradation. The decline may not be visible yet, but it's on the way. As we talk about Existers and Diminishers in this context, it's important to note Existers don't usually remain that way forever. Unless something awakens them to the journey of becoming an Improver, over time, Existers eventually devolve into Diminishers. While you may think you or your organization is treading water, in truth, you're either growing or declining, and this is a sobering thought when you consider the implications.

I heard someone say recently in the context of being married, "You're either working on your marriage, or you're working on your divorce." Same idea; whether we're talking marriage, parenting, fitness, money management, or any other domain of life, you've got to work and make adjustments to thrive.

For an individual, adapting means being willing to learn innovative ideas, evolve your positions, and hone new skills. It requires spending time observing, reflecting, and pondering the current and potential future circumstances, altering your position as needed to fit the situation. It may sound a little cheesy to say aloud with all the rhyming words, but if you're not willing to reset your mindset, you're going to be upset.

→ *Consider this:* If you were to "reset" an area of your life, which action or habit would have the most positive impact?

You may be familiar with Abraham Maslow's Four Stages of Learning,[61] which are:

1. Unconscious Incompetence - We don't know that we don't know.
2. Conscious Incompetence - We know that we don't know.
3. Conscious Competence - We work at what we don't know.
4. Unconscious Competence - We don't have to think about knowing it.

The Improver is willing to take the journey from unconscious *incompetence* to unconscious *competence* as many times as it takes. This is needed because the thing we were once convinced of was true, *was* true, or accepted as true at the time, but is true no longer. In other words, we are aware that we each have cognitive biases, where what we think we know is wrong or outdated, but we will not let them keep us from being open to new ideas and perspectives.

The Covid pandemic brought this to plain sight as we heard the word *pivot* everywhere we turned. But it doesn't take an outbreak for us to cause a need to pivot. Markets fluctuate. Companies become disruptors. New inventions change the landscape. Technology gets updated. Culture and society change. Kids grow up and move out (hopefully!). All these variables mean we must be responsibly reactive to the world around us if we want to win. We must be open-minded and understand when to update our positions. Improvers see these transitions as opportunities rather than threats.

Mark Twain once said, "What gets us into trouble is not what we don't know. It's what we know for sure that just ain't so."[62]

Have you ever held a strong position or belief only to later find out you were wrong? It can be tough to admit when our view of reality is challenged. A poll by the University of New Hampshire in 2021 revealed approximately 10% of Americans still believe the earth is flat.[63] (Facepalm.)

Even in the face of undeniable facts and evidence, some people will always choose to hold to their ill-informed opinions. I remember hearing growing up, "It's easier to sel a lie than to give away the truth." People can be strangely resistant to new information, regardless of its veracity. The Improver, while steadfast and faithful, should not be stubborn or foolish.

I know it's fashionable to say, "Never give up," but sometimes you should. I've given up lots of things in life and business (and so have you). There were times when I decided to roll out a new service or implement an idea followed by receiving feedback (usually in the form of negative ROI!) showing me how stupid my decision was. You bet I gave up! At least on that iteration or version.

That said, Improvers must discern when we are being adaptable vs when we are being fickle. I've known people to tuck tail and run when the going gets tough or deviate from the course when facing any resistance. That's not being flexible; it's being fearful. Vision, prayer, and wisdom are needed to help you know when to stand strong and push forward, or when you should change your approach. So, I'll implore you to stay the course, but only if you're going in the right direction.

CHOOSE TO WIN

As I was in the early days of my personal growth journey, I was introduced to the great teachings of Zig Ziglar. Zig was one of the most powerful motivators ever to walk the planet, and his life was characterized by a charisma that drew others to him by the thousands.

His son, Tom Ziglar, has continued Zig's amazing legacy, so I was incredibly excited when he and I were on a podcast together. During our discussion, he talked about his book "Choose to Win," where he encourages readers to commit to being a winner by replacing bad habits with good habits, thereby making the most of their life. The book's premise is that "the fastest way to success is to replace a bad habit with a good habit."[64] In other words, you must be willing to change and adapt to create new success.

Yes, replacing habits is difficult, and yes, change can be uncomfortable. Be encouraged—the more time you proactively spend outside of your comfort zone, the more time you'll get to spend inside of it. As Dave Ramsey says about making improvements on your spending, giving, and saving, "Live like no one else (now), so later you can live like no one else."[5]

At the end of the day, what got you here won't get you there. Yes, you've made it this far, but if you want to be an Improver, you'll need to be willing and able to change. The ability to rethink what feels already settled in our minds is paramount to winning. For the Christian, Romans 12:2 tells us that we should be transformed by the renewing of our minds. When we allow our minds to be renewed, it results in change. And this change isn't just for us; it's for those in our circles of influence where we live, learn, work, and play.

BENDS IN THE ROAD

We mentioned Mark Twain earlier in the chapter. Fun fact: one of his friends was none other than Helen Keller, the world-famous author and activist. At age two, Keller became deaf and blind, living in a world of quietness and darkness. If you want to see a shining example of an individual who could adapt, you'd be hard-pressed to find someone with the resolve of Keller. Despite her physical handicaps, she learned to read, write, and even earn a college degree.

Overcoming doubt, discouragement, and "disabilities," she is a model for what can be accomplished if one is willing to do whatever it takes to win. One of my favorite quotes from her is, "A bend in the road is not the end of the road unless you fail to make the turn."[66]

Bends in your road are coming. Will you make the turn?

Assuming you are indeed prepared to make the turn, then you're truly taking on the mentality of an Improver, and I applaud you.

Being ready and willing to change is only part of the way there, however. The other part requires applying the *Daily High Five* and creating the environment for change to be practical, beneficial, and celebrated. It means taking on a mentality of habitual reflection, continuous learning, and rebounding from failure. (Pro-tip: Read biographies and autobiographies of people who have experienced astounding transformation journeys of their own. Their inspiration will be fuel for your own growth.)

Even after doing all you can do, our hope and desire for positive outcomes can fall short, leaving us disappointed, confused, and frustrated. Sometimes our willpower is not powerful enough. This is why it's important to know that our ultimate source of positive transformation is from our Creator and Sustainer.

The Bible gives many images of God changing us for good, including refining us like gold and silver in a fire and molding us like clay. He is sanctifying us in each season, making us more pure and more in line with who we are meant to be. In Romans we are encouraged that we can be transformed by "renewing our mind." Improver, if you're willing to change, but struggling with actually making change, then seek the One who knows you and your situation best. There's no greater way for the Improver to improve than through the One who is already perfect and willing to help make us better, if only we are willing.

KEY POINTS

1. For the Improver to enjoy long-term success, whether in life or business, he must adapt and innovate.
2. The key to adaptability is the right mindset, which begins with a willingness to change.
3. Change is most powerfully experienced through seeking help from our Creator.

QUESTIONS FOR REFLECTION (GOOD)

1. When was a time that you responded effectively to new circumstances?
2. How have you demonstrated flexibility in your areas of responsibility?
3. When/where have you helped others successfully adjust and adapt?

QUESTIONS FOR DIRECTION (GETTIN' BETTER)

1. How might you anticipate disruptions and deviations in the future and better respond to them?
2. What area of your life or business do you need to invest in and bring up to date?
3. How can you help those others improve by staying relevant and adapting to change?

CHAPTER 10:
MAKING THE MOVE

"Get action. Do things; be sane; don't fritter away your time; create, act, take a place wherever you are and be somebody; get action."
— Theodore Roosevelt

My wife Kathryn and I had a conversation while we were still dating. As they like to say, things were getting serious. She made a simple statement that made a significant impression. While on the topic of our Christian faith, she said, "I'll tell you this right now; I'm not signing up to marry a bench warmer. I expect you to be in the game."

What?! The phrasing and tone took me a moment to comprehend.

I never was one of the jock kind of guys, so I knew she wasn't referring to me becoming the star QB of the local football team! No, she was making a point – faith was important to her, and if we were to be together, I'd have to bring a certain level of energy and action to the table.

It wasn't enough to avoid being a Diminisher that would hinder her faith; I couldn't be an Exister just casually tolerating it either. She wanted me in the game improving the game, not sitting on the bench observing others doing the heavy lifting. I would need to take action.

Taking action and getting moving is what this chapter is about. Talk is cheap. Dreaming is easy. Improvers get moving and get stuff done.

A MAN'S MAN

There are a handful of rugged guys who come to mind when I think of what it means to be a "man's man." One of those guys is Jack London (aka John Griffith Chaney). His famous books, *The Call of the Wild* and *White Fang*, were inspirations to me as a boy. (Probably because he was so favorable to being the underdog, which I related to personally.)

In the Call of the Wild, he posits, "The proper function of a man is to live, not to exist. I shall not waste my days in trying to prolong them. I shall use my time."[67]

That's the sentiment we're after here; living to the full, not existing in the minimum.

Another man, Philo Buck, was an academic who became intrigued by this adventurous outlook on life, so he included Jack in his survey of successful people. Jack writes to Philo in 1913,

> "Please remember I am talking about the world as it is. The men who act without thinking, and the men who both think and act, are the ones who mold

the world. The man who thinks and does not act never molds the world. He may think that he does — but that, too, is only a thought, the thought of a deedless, actionless thinker."[68]

You cannot be an Improver and an actionless thinker at the same time. Forward progress requires positive effort and movement. One of the ways I define success is hearing "Well done, good and faithful servant..."[69] from my heavenly Father once I pass from this life into the next. Did you catch a keyword there – "done." Eternity's welcome will not be "well said," "well thought out," "well discussed," or "well imagined." James reminds us that "faith **without works** is dead."[70] (Emphasis mine.) Action is key. Be a doer, not just an observer or listener.

RELEASE THE BREAKS

Going forward requires conscious effort. The issue isn't that most people don't *want* to begin. The trouble is that often we drive through life with our psychological brakes on. These brakes can be a variety of things, but are typically negative images about yourself, inaccurate beliefs about reality, guilt, and self-doubt. These brakes cancel out your good intentions, no matter how hard you try to move your goals forward.

Successful people learn to release the brakes. They overcome their fear, choose to see reality, and affirm positivity in their life. Just like when you learned to drive, you can't have your foot on both the brake and gas pedal at the same time and expect progress.

Movement in the vehicle isn't going to happen until the driver firmly decides to go somewhere. Are you ready to go somewhere? Do you have hopes and dreams and goals and aspirations? I want you to make the decision that you're about to go somewhere.

You don't have to decide exactly *where* you're going yet. Just decide *that* you are going to move from Point A to Point B. You're going to take a chance. You are going to improve something. You'll have to overcome some challenges along the way, but the first thing you're going to have to do is decide to act.

There's an insightful moment in *Pride and Prejudice* in which Darcy tells of his challenges and inhibitions interacting socially followed by Elizabeth offering her rebuttal:

"I certainly have not the talent which some people possess," said Darcy, "of conversing easily with those I have never seen before. I cannot catch their tone of conversation, or appear interested in their concerns, as I often see done."

"My fingers," said Elizabeth, "do not move over this instrument in the masterly manner which I see so many women's do. They have not the same force or rapidity, and do not produce the same expression. But then I have always supposed it to be my own fault—because I would not take the trouble of practicing. It is not that I do not believe my fingers as capable as any other woman's of superior execution."

"You are perfectly right," replied Darcy. "You have employed your time much better."[71]

In this scene, Darcy abdicated any responsibility for his lack of social etiquette and relational connection, while Elizabeth acknowledged that any shortcomings in her ability to play the piano were a consequence of her decision to not practice more. For some of us, we are Darcy, relegating ourselves to what we think is our natural way. Others, like Elizabeth, acknowledge that change is possible, but it requires conscious effort, movement, and practice. So, don't fret if you're not a master at socializing, playing the piano, or any other ambition. Just get started and initiate momentum in the right direction.

ROPES COURSE

When I was leading a youth ministry in Northeast Louisiana, I took my key leaders to an outdoor ropes course at a recreational encampment called Seeker Springs. I thought it would be good for them to get out of their comfort zone and do something risky and challenging.

We faced one exciting obstacle on the course that included two electrical poles about 50 feet tall connected by two sets of cabling stretched horizontally (connecting the two vertical poles). One of those horizontal cables is intended for you to put your feet on while the other one about 10 feet higher is the one your safety harness is attached to in case you fall. That top cable also has ropes dangling from it every few feet so that you'll have a handle for balance.

The objective is to climb the pole, use the ropes in hand and cable under the feet to go sideways across the cabling to the other side, and ride the zip line down. This seemed simple enough, and our leaders began one by one making their way through it with relative ease.

Then it was my turn. I climbed the pole. Put my feet on the cable and grabbed the first rope. So far, so good. But I have a slight fear of heights, and my vertigo was increasing. As I reached for the second rope with my left hand, my right hand was still clinging to the first rope. Now, here's where it gets funky. The people who built this course spread the ropes' width far enough apart that it's almost impossible to grab the next rope without releasing your current one.

I returned safely to my "home rope." I tried to reach my next rope a couple more times while staying tethered, but I couldn't. My heart rate was increasing, my knees were beginning to wobble, and my mind was full of regret for trying this ridiculous team-building exercise. (I still get a little anxious thinking about this event!)

Meanwhile, the rest of the group is cheering for me down below. It took what seemed like an eternity to gather the courage to let go, dispel my fears, and move forward, but I finally did it. Yay! What I thought would be a stretch moment for my team ended up being a growth moment for me.

Here's the point: Sometimes, we have to decide to let go of what we're holding on to even though we don't have our next handle yet. It feels scary. You don't have control. You can't see the solution yet. You're like Indiana Jones in *The Last Crusade*,[72] taking that step of faith over the big abyss. It doesn't make sense. You don't know how it'll work out, but to improve, you have to move.

THE FALSE PROMISE OF HUSTLE

Not acting is one end of the spectrum to avoid; the other extreme is moving and working incessantly, making it all about the hustle. Healthy Improvers are not workaholics. Yes, Improvers know when it's time to roll up their sleeves and get to work, but that's not the same thing as believing that just grinding it out always leads to success. Some people think that the only way to win is through non-stop blood, sweat, and tears—pull yourself up by the bootstraps and all that. Hustle culture is a trap.

When I first got into business, I was recommended to an inspirational life-coach figure whose whole premise and tagline was, "Sleep is for suckers." You don't get to rest. You don't get to have a life. You must work and work and work, and if you work long enough, if you work hard enough, if you've got enough grit, then eventually, maybe you can realize your ambitions.

I strongly disagree with that philosophy. I have a family now. I have a purpose now. I don't want to wait to start living. Of course, there are seasons where you do invest more in certain areas, like your education or career, than other seasons, but if you work efficiently and effectively, you can find a healthy balance (and get some sleep in the process).

Work is a good thing. What a blessing to be able to labor in a way that offers a product or service to the world while providing for the needs of you and your family. Work is good, but work is not God; don't worship it.

SUPERFICIAL PRODUCTIVITY

A salesman from a rural town once told me, "I'm busier than a cat on a hot tin roof." While slightly amused, I didn't find it respectable. This guy was all over the place, frazzled, and unfocused. In and of itself, busyness is not an indicator of success, integrity, or an honorable job. I understand it's somewhat fashionable to tell people how busy we are, but *busyness* is not *business*.

The talent market for hiring can be challenging at times, in part because most people are used to being paid for being available and being active. I always tell our applicants, "We don't pay for activity and availability – we pay for productivity." We want to see meaningful progress towards our vision and goals. We want to see the ball being pushed down the field. As Henry David Thoreau said, "It is not enough to be busy. So are the ants. The question is: What are we busy about?"[73]

→ *Consider this:* Is there something you have been working incredibly hard on and investing a lot of time and resources into that isn't truly productive or meaningful? Is it time to let it go?

People don't always want to hear that kind of talk, however, because work that matters to the bottom line and is truly productive is often hard and uncomfortable. Comfort kills growth. You can be crazy busy and still be lazy if you only do what is easy and comfortable.

READY, AIM, FIRE

If productivity is not activity, busyness, or grinding, what is it? Productivity is progress towards your vision and goals at a pace that is sustainable for the long term. Michael Hyatt says it this way, "Productivity is not about getting *more* things done; it's about getting the *right* things done."[74]

"Ready, aim, fire" is the right rhythm when attempting to hit your target. This is not just true in firearms, but in home and workplace settings as well. There is a rhythm to hitting the bullseye and the rhythm is a certain pace of getting ready, aiming, and pulling the trigger.

Personally, where I tend to go wrong as an Improver is wanting everything to be perfect, so I aim...aim...aim... just fire already! I overthink decisions. I plan out details that don't matter. I delay putting something out until I think it's just perfect. This book has taken years to write, mostly because of my tendency to keep aiming, wanting everything to be exact.

Meanwhile, I have friends who are more akin to Yosemite Sam (remember him from Looney Tunes?). They come in hot, guns blazing. Bang, bang, bang! They typically hit the targets more than me, but they also miss more than me. And sometimes, when they miss, they cause injury or damage. As much as we want to avoid indefinitely delaying for the perfect shot, we also want to avoid indiscriminately firing at will.

It's a tough balance taking action at the right rhythm, but that's what the Improver does. What is the right shot that will get us close to the real target? Once it feels right, don't overthink it, go for it.

Proverbs 31 tells of a noble wife who "considers a field and buys it...sets about her work vigorously...watches over the affairs of her household and does not eat the bread of idleness..."[75] She considers, then acts. She oversees her responsibilities and *works* on her tasks. No idling or wasting away time. This is the way.

Are you sitting on something that you need to act on? Are you waiting for the opportune time?

A friend of mine told me several years ago, "A good something is better than a best nothing." That grammar is a little off, but the sentiment is true. I've had lots of "best nothings," ideas that were perfected mentally and never actioned, plans mulled over and refined and not expressed. The difference between the average person and the entrepreneurs who create something and make it big isn't usually the idea itself. People have million-dollar ideas every day, but only a few people take action on them.

To be the Improver you were meant to be, you need to get moving. It's like my old football coach used to say when he wanted to motivate us, "I'm looking for more than just warm bodies!" His encouragement is my encouragement: stop taking up space and passively observing everyone else take action. Don't be like an Exister - go live, learn, work, and play like an Improver and make something better.

As poet William Woodsworth put it, "To begin, *begin.*"[76]

KEY POINTS

1. Because Improvers desire to make things better, they can't be paralyzed but must choose to take action and get to work.
2. Overworking or unfocused work isn't productive or admirable.
3. Improvers consider the best course forward and take purposeful action without delay.

QUESTIONS FOR REFLECTION (GOOD)

1. What is an area of your life or work where you have taken bold action?
2. Where do you feel you have a good balance and/or healthy boundaries?
3. What are you most proud of lately, whether personal or professional?

QUESTIONS FOR DIRECTION (GETTIN' BETTER)

1. What are you procrastinating on or delaying that needs action?
2. Where do you need to speed up or slow down?
3. What is keeping you busy, but isn't productive for your goals?

CHAPTER 11

WINNING WITH INTEGRITY

"Do not consider anything for your interest which makes you break your word, quit your modesty, or inclines you to any practice which will not bear the light, or look the world in the face."
— *Marcus Aurelius*

Early in the launch of my insurance agency business in 2015, I was on the phone following up with a prospect who happened to be the oldest potential client I had ever attempted to help. We'll call him Mr. James.

Mr. James was nearly 90 years old and was an absolute joy to talk with. The process thus far had gone swimmingly, and under normal circumstances, I would have assumed the sale was already a done deal. Yet, I could ascertain by the tone of his voice and his general hesitancy that something was holding him back. A key part of our conversation went something like this:

"Mr. James, it seems to me that we have answered all our questions and have found a solution that improves your coverage while lowering your premium. You're getting everything you were looking for, but you have yet to pull the trigger on the new policy. May I ask what's holding you back?"

In his gentle yet strong voice, he said, "Well, son, all this does sound pretty good, and I appreciate all you've done to help me out here. But the thing is, I've not seen you eyeball to eyeball. I've never shaken your hand. Over the phone, it's hard to know what kind of man you are. I keep asking myself a question, so I'll just come out and ask you: How do I know I can trust you?"

I was slightly taken aback by the question since no one had ever asked me that before. I was also a little stunned because I had prepared responses to almost any objection or question a prospect could pose. Mr. James, however, in his brutal honesty, had put me in the unusual spot of being speechless.

After a few seconds to regain my thoughts and reflect briefly, I replied, "Mr. James, thank you for asking that question. I've never had anyone ask me that before. Come to think of it, I've probably taken most people's trust for granted. That said, would you like me to answer in a professional and polished way or just tell you what's really on my mind?"

"Shoot straight with me," he said.

"Well," I replied, "part of my belief about life is that one of these days, I'm going to breathe my last breath. I'll be put into a wooden box and lowered about 6 feet under. My personal belief is that I will be face-to-face with the Creator of the universe giving an account for the good and bad I did in this world. Mr. James, my bad list is already long enough, and I don't need your insurance policy on it!"

He had a hearty laugh at my response and, while catching his breath, told me to sign him up. After I hung up the phone call, I wondered where the word picture idea had come from. I had never thought of it quite that way, nor had anyone else explained their philosophy to me in such a manner.

The closest connection I could make was from Matthew 5:14-29. In this passage, Jesus tells the Parable of the Talents, which is about a man who entrusts his property to three of his servants before going on a journey. Each servant receives a different number of talents (a form of currency) according to their ability. Two of the servants faithfully multiplied what was entrusted to them, while one fearfully hid his. Upon the master's return, he evaluates their stewardship based on how they have used their talents. Before rebuking the one who managed out of fear, the master affirms the two who increased their holdings and stewarded their resources well by saying, "Well done, good and faithful servant! You were faithful over a few things; I will put you in charge of many things. Share your master's joy.'"

This parable offers a paradigm for how we should view this life and the next. We have been entrusted with a certain number of resources, including our abilities, skills, and financial assets. We must manage these until the day comes when we pass on from this earth to face our Master and give an account of how well we steward-ed what He put into our care.

As I thought about the application of the parable, I made the conscious decision at that moment that I would forever strive to run my business and manage my affairs with the mindset that one day, I would be accountable for my actions. Regardless of who is watching or what the circumstances are, it will always be my priority to do the right thing for each person I serve. Like the faithful stew-ards in the parable, I hope one day to hear, "Well done, good and faithful servant!"

My belief about what happens after death carries significant weight in the way I live my life. Likewise, what you believe and value in life and about life matters. What is most important to you will shape your decisions and actions. It determines how you interact with others and operate your affairs. An Improver lives with a high sense of responsibility and firm principles which results in uncom-promising integrity.

INTEGRITY RED ALERTS

Integrity is such a buzzword that almost every compa-ny has it listed somewhere in their values or vision state-ments. Some even have the word *integrity* as their brand. Ask any crowd to list the characteristics of a good leader, and you'll get integrity in the top three responses. Yet, for all its fanfare, when you survey the world around us, it seems like integrity is in short supply. Being held responsi-ble and showing firm convictions and principles has ap-parently become old-fashioned.

While this chapter was being written, three prominent pastors in the Dallas-Fort Worth metroplex resigned due to accusations of moral misconduct, one of which involved sexual abuse of a 12-year-old girl. It seems even the most (apparently) upright, reputable, and morally knowledgeable people in our society are not protected from failures of integrity. To some degree, we all have the potential to fall prey to a significant lapse in judgment, and we must always be on guard because our adversary is consistently seeking to attack us (1 Peter 5:8-9).

What causes someone to lose integrity? Why would someone choose to swindle a company out of money, cheat on their spouse, or defraud an innocent person? What are the factors that could lead you to compromise on your core convictions and values?

Red Alert is a 1958 novel about nuclear war and avoiding catastrophe. The story highlights how one bomb can destroy what took many years to build, creating a ripple effect of pain and destruction.[77] In the same way that a chemical explosion can demolish entire cities, a personal integrity breakdown in your life can bring down in a moment all you have worked hard to achieve and have dire consequences for others. The good news is that certain risk factors sound an alarm when the chance of danger is prevalent. If we recognize these "red alerts," we can act against the threats and keep our integrity intact.

These red alerts are:

1. Pressure to Succeed
2. Lack of Moral Clarity
3. Desire for Others' Approval

4. Stress and Emotional Strain
5. Missing Support System

INTEGRITY RED ALERTS

When any number of these red alerts are present in our lives, we should be on guard. Becoming familiar with them will help us build our own "Spidey sense" to warn us of impending danger.

RED ALERT #1 - PRESSURE TO SUCCEED

When the desire to achieve success, whether in a professional or personal context, becomes overwhelming, individuals may compromise their integrity to reach their goals. The temptation of personal gain, such as financial rewards, power, or status, can pull us away from our center and lead us to act against our moral principles and values. I've seen this time and time again in the sales arena where an account executive or business development manager is pushing hard to reach their quota. To hit their target, they mislead the client, omit information, or misrepresent the deal.

In 2019, the "Operation Varsity Blues'' scandal erupted. The conspiracy came to light after it was revealed that over fifty individuals, including prominent leaders, celebrities, and college coaches had manipulated the college admissions process to get children into prestigious universities. Unethical tactics, like falsifying athletic profiles for high-profile player prospects, were used to manipulate the process. Millions of dollars of fraud activity transacted all because a select group of parents and leaders buckled under elitism and chose a superficial view of success.

At some point in our professional journeys, most of us have been forced to face the potential of negative outcomes such as losing a job, getting demoted, or missing a bonus, but we cannot use these circumstances to compromise our integrity. The pressure to succeed (or avoid failure) has caused the downfall of many good people, and if you feel this pressure beginning to build, be on your guard.

RED ALERT #2 - LACK OF MORAL CLARITY

My family has been known to use a humorous moniker when describing my ability to rationalize my bad decisions. They tell me that I'm "justin-fying" my actions! While this is usually done in jest, there is a hint of truth to my effort to feel justified when I mess up. And while the one-off excuse here and there may not be a big deal, a habit of casually excusing errors can lead to a more significant compromise of integrity.

Show me someone who never admits wrong, always passes the blame, and never takes responsibility, and I can assure you that person lacks integrity. They muddy the waters morally so that rules and expectations can be adapted to their benefit. Unethical behavior thrives when a person has ambiguity or confusion about what is right and wrong.

Often people in these situations are asking the wrong questions:

— What do I want?
— What would make me popular?
— What will I settle for?
— What is technically allowed by the rules?
— What will the stakeholders think?
— What are other people doing?
— What is easiest?

Instead of these types of questions, moral clarity asks, "What is the good and right decision here?" This is a question that leads to wisdom. Believers who are consistently engaged in the Bible have an advantage here, because the Scriptures are a constant reminder of the moral values and duties that God has prescribed. Although everything is not always black-and-white, those who know the foundation of their ethics have a high chance of not being shaken.

As the old saying goes, "If you don't stand for something, you'll fall for anything." The Improver must be clear about his morals and stand firmly on values and principles so he can avoid falling into temptation.

RED ALERT #3 - DESIRE FOR OTHERS' APPROVAL

Seeking validation or approval from others, especially from those in positions of authority or influence, is a major contributor that can lead to compromising one's integrity. Although I learned of peer pressure early in life, I still underestimated the influence of peers and social groups. The need to compromise my standards has been most strongly felt in environments where I look to gain favor or acceptance. I say and do things I'd normally never say or do.

In my early 20's, I was invited to speak at a church fundraiser for a friend, who was also my employer. I was honored by the invitation but also a little nervous about it. This was a predominantly African-American church with different customs, music, and styles that I was not accustomed to. I'm embarrassed to say that my message that day was more about gaining amens and applause than it was about serving my friend and his congregation. I just wanted to be accepted and feel included, so I pandered on my values and squandered an opportunity.

Our internal alarm system should begin sounding when we feel a strong fear of rejection and a compelling desire for approval and acceptance. The Improver keeps this red alert from being set off by setting boundaries, building confidence, and thinking through the consequences of falling prey to the wishes of others.

RED ALERT #4 - STRESS AND EMOTIONAL STRAIN

Elevated levels of stress or emotional strain can impair judgment and lead to decisions that compromise integrity. Stress comes in a variety of areas:

- financial
- physical
- social
- marital
- parental
- professional
- mental
- emotional

The word "stress" has a negative connotation, but healthy amounts of stress can be motivating, empowering, and clarifying. The problem is when our light-to-moderate stress becomes more extreme, and the weight of it impairs our judgment and leaves our integrity in danger of negative impact. In Chapter 4 we talked about the principles of growing healthy, which includes Implementing the *Improver Planning System* so you can reduce and manage stress more effectively over time.

One example of this danger was during the Covid-19 pandemic and the unprecedented stress placed on healthcare workers, including doctors, nurses, and support staff. They were thrust into the frontlines of the crisis, facing immense physical, mental and emotional strain. As the pandemic spread and the stress increased, healthcare workers found themselves overworked and overwhelmed.

The impact of this was palpable and devastating for many. Stories surfaced of exhausted nurses administering the wrong medication or overlooking critical symptoms. Although not every situation was intentional, the integrity of the care was compromised. Once organizations and governments implemented measures to manage stress and support the workers, these negative incidents were significantly reduced.

You may not ever be a healthcare worker on the frontlines of a pandemic, but the chances are you will, at some season of your life, find yourself facing high levels of stress in many areas. Be aware of your stress levels, and recognize when they begin to rise as a potential danger zone.

RED ALERT #5 - MISSING SUPPORT SYSTEM

Few factors risk our wholeness more than not having people around us to keep us on track. Like a car out of alignment, each of us, left to our own devices, has the propensity to veer away from the right path. Although Red Alert #3 reminds us that others can pressure us to negatively compromise who we are, when we are in healthy circles of relationships, the opposite is true. Those around us can help us be more virtuous versions of ourselves.

In our coaching and consulting company, we give a lot of attention to the topic of your inner circle and core relationships because the ramifications are so significant. God has created us to live in community and support one another. When we isolate ourselves and don't have the proper support systems, we become the most vulnerable. When there is little or no accountability for actions, individuals may feel emboldened to act without integrity.

These five red alerts serve as warning signals to us. When we notice any of these creeping into our lives, personally or professionally, we must raise our guard and diligently work to safeguard our integrity.

MINDSET CHECKER

In addition to having a significant effect on our principles and values, viewing winning through the lens of eternity shifts our priorities and mindset. Knowing there is more to life than the naturalistic things we observe around us should cause us to think about what matters most. Believing some things are temporal and some are eternal, our focus should be on the eternal.

Perspective often comes down to a matter of choice. Our mindset and attitude are almost always within our control. On the eve of my last birthday, I remember feeling this overbearing sense of imposter syndrome. I was gathering feedback on book subtitles (for this book) and many of the phrases had to do with "moving beyond a life of insignificance."

During this same time frame, an internal problem surfaced for me as I suddenly realized I had zero plans for my birthday with anyone outside of my direct family. No friend gatherings. No work-related get-togethers. I'm not sure what was different that year, but outside of my wife and kids, I wasn't connecting with anyone for my birthday. And let's face it, my family is obligated to celebrate me.

There I was, supposedly writing a book about living a life of impact and significance, yet I couldn't even clear the extremely low bar of being invited to breakfast, coffee, or lunch on my birthday. For someone who views themselves as being connected and a leader of others, the emotions of smallness and isolation were heavy. I felt like an egotistical hypocrite for having the audacity to author a book on a topic I clearly wasn't qualified to discuss.

My pity party did not last long, however. I became convicted about my negative thoughts and began to call them out. I acknowledged the short-sighted positions I had chosen to take and decided to change my attitude. Once I changed my perspective, my emotions and actions followed suit.

I decided to write down these competing mindsets and review them from time to time to make sure I was remaining in the right headspace. This list would become the *Improver Mindset Checker*, which is a helpful tool to reflect on whether we are in the right mental space and provide guardrails if we are veering off track. Our default mindset is the one that comes most naturally to us and puts us squarely in the Exister or Diminisher way of thinking and living. The Improver mindset, on the other hand, helps us to take our thoughts captive and choose a perspective that will lead to greater things.

Take a moment to consider your circumstances and check which boxes on each side best describe your current mentality. As much as possible, objectively evaluate yourself against the *Improver Mindset Checker*.

IMPROVER MINDSET CHECKER

DEFAULT MINDSET · IMPROVER MINDSET

☐ CRITICIZER ——————→ ☐ CREATOR

☐ CONSUMER ——————→ ☐ INVESTOR

☐ VICTIM ——————→ ☐ VICTOR

☐ OVERWHELMED ——————→ ☐ OVERCOMING

☐ OBSTACLE ——————→ ☐ OPPORTUNITY

☐ FIXED ——————→ ☐ GROWTH

☐ SCARCITY ——————→ ☐ ABUNDANCE

☐ FEAR ——————→ ☐ FAITH

☐ PROBLEMS ——————→ ☐ POSSIBILITIES

☐ ENVY ——————→ ☐ GRATITUDE

It's worth repeating that you can't always control what happens to you, but you can control your response to it. By positively adjusting your attitude and seeking redemption in your situation, what seemed like a burden can become a blessing. And sometimes that blessing is for others. Often, your struggle becomes your story. Your pain becomes a platform. Your mess becomes a message. And your biggest test becomes your biggest testimony.

And this is what winning well looks like. It's a person who chooses the right mindset and right actions regardless of circumstance; someone that can stare the challenge in the face and still act with courage and boldness of heart.

I once thought about getting a personalized license plate, "Just Wins." That phrase represents the first four letters of my first and last name (Justin Winstead). When I mentioned it to my pastor, he really liked the idea and affectionately nicknamed me "Just Wins."

One day, the literal application of those words dawned on me vividly. "Just" means honest, good, right, and principled. And "wins" means to be victorious, come out on top, achieve, and prevail. The interpretative meaning of *just wins* is how an Improver views integrity. It's a mentality of winning, triumph, and prevailing, *but* in a manner and method that is worthy, principled, and true. That's what I hope for you—to really enjoy progress and success because the basis of it is good and right. I pray your life would be marked by *just wins*.

At the core, that's what this book is about - taking on the best mindset possible to become the healthiest versions of ourselves, so we can live life more fully and leave a lasting legacy of impact. An Improver keeps the big picture of eternity in mind when making decisions, interacting with people, and responding to situations. We long to hear the words "well done" as we win the game of life with integrity.

KEY POINTS

1. Winning without integrity isn't really winning.
2. Five indicators alert us to potential integrity failures. These include pressure to succeed, lack of moral clarity, desire for others' approval, stress and emotional strain, and a missing support system.
3. To achieve true success, we must override our default mindset with an Improver mindset.

QUESTIONS FOR REFLECTION (GOOD)

1. When did you successfully overcome a temptation to compromise your integrity?
2. In what ways have you been a moral support system for others?
3. What items in the mindset checker are currently healthy and productive for you?

QUESTIONS FOR DIRECTION (GETTIN' BETTER)

1. What "red alerts" have you noticed in your life that signal a potential compromise of integrity?
2. What steps can you take to cultivate a support system that helps uphold your integrity?
3. In what areas of your life can you prioritize eternal perspectives over immediate gains?

CHAPTER 12:

A TRANSFORMATION FABLE

W e are ending this book on becoming an Improver with a story. It is a fictional tale, but it's based on real-life people and situations, particularly connected to the entrepreneurs and small business/organization leaders I am privileged to serve on a regular basis. This transformation fable will illustrate many of the points and principles found throughout the other chapters and hopefully bring clarity and inspiration to you.

At the conclusion of this chapter is an invitation for you to create your own real-life transformation story by accepting the invitation to become an Improver. So let's finish strong here and get ready to get better.

JACOB'S STORY

Jacob Coleman is an ambitious professional hired a few years ago for what many would consider an ideal job at a reputable firm. The salary and benefits and the apparent permanence of a stable company created an environment for Jacob to get his life going. After joining the company upon completing his undergraduate degree, he married and bought a house, which was soon filled with energetic kids and the family dog.

Attending a local church and taking part in sports and community events, Jacob, from all appearances, was living the life he'd always imagined and had everything going for him. Yet, on the inside, Jacob was yearning for more—*Is this it? Is there something more?* He also knew that life was missing that extra pizzazz he used to enjoy.

As Jacob continued his commute to and from the office, clocking in and out, he became increasingly convinced that he felt pulled to something greater. Knowing he wasn't reaching his potential and desiring more freedom and autonomy, Jacob considered being his own boss. Surely, he could run his business well instead of working for someone else's dream.

Perhaps he could even be one of the incredible entrepreneurs who creates something unique that changes the world and makes more money than he ever fathomed. He could change his family tree! But he knew he wouldn't compromise his integrity like many other greedy businessmen he'd observed from afar. No, he'd give to his church and community to make a difference, and as importantly, he would be available and present for his family and kids.

Jacob promised himself if ever given the opportunity, he'd be the husband he longed to be, the dad he didn't have growing up, and the kind of business leader others could respect and follow.

The day finally came when Jacob had had enough. The company just didn't get it, and worse, it didn't care. He could sense he had hit his ceiling there, and the ' rat race" had grown wearisome.

His family savings were enough so that he could leave the job and not face any immediate negative financial consequences. Coincidentally, he had recently heard about a family friend who was selling his pool services company close to his home. There was already a decent client base (although not enough to support his family and lifestyle), and the sale would include most of the tools he needed to succeed.

It wasn't the new and edgy business he had imagined, especially after watching all those "Shark Tank" episodes. On top of that, there was no unique, patented idea he could call his own, but it was nevertheless attractive. All the support and structure of an existing operation with the perks of being in charge of his business!

Since leaving his employer, Jacob had experienced a whirlwind of fast-moving events. He quickly obtained training and completed an array of documents to rebrand to his own liking. These were exciting times: imagining the potential of his business, picking the perfect office location, purchasing the marketing materials and signage (with his name prominently displayed), and telling his friends and family about his bold move—he was legit! Everyone was supportive and affirming, and Jacob became convinced this was the beginning of a brand-new life. And he was correct.

Before he knew it, Jacob already had more home-owners calling for quotes, including some (but confusingly to him, not all) of his closest friends and family. He was surprised at those who gave him a chance after his new business launch and equally shocked by those who didn't. Even still, having done better than he expected with navigating the technical nuances of the trade, it was pleasing to see the early fruit of his labor.

Quick calculations revealed the potential for future earnings, and it hit him, "This thing actually works!" The work was challenging and exciting (even fun?) AND he was getting paid to do it; Jacob was off to the races.

The calendar became filled with phone calls, coffee meetings, networking and marketing events, and workshops and training classes. Every day was a new challenge. As the hours built, so did his client base. He was well on his way to creating a thriving business.

Jacob was shocked at how busy he was. At some point in the beginning, he wondered whether he would find enough customers to connect with his business, but to his surprise, the days were increasingly overloaded with sales calls and appointments. The other tasks of running the company, such as financials, reporting, and data entry, began to spill over to the evenings and weekends. He was away from the family more than he intended, and his health and personal friendships had taken a minor hit, yet he was making noteworthy progress. Deep down, he knew this was temporary, or at least he hoped it was.

As the long days turned into long quarters, which turned into fleeting years, Jacob was gaining clients but losing steam. The emotional high of launching a business had long worn off. The family, though always supportive, was largely disconnected from his success. Though their family budget had increased, there was no proportional shift in their happiness or closeness.

The new friendships he had forged in exchange for the old ones did not seem as deep or long-lasting. To add insult to injury, the business meetings over food and drinks and extended time at the desk had led to the dreaded two-punch combo of weight gain and back pain. Jacob's dad always said, "When the going gets tough, you get tougher." So, Jacob powered through. One foot in front of the other, he journeyed on.

No one had warned Jacob about the uncanny unpredictability of business. In one sense, he knew all businesses were volatile, and certainly a couple of seasoned professionals may have mentioned being ready for "highs and lows," but no one had prepared him for treacherous waves that would cause him to question the very purpose of what he was doing and why.

The advancement of his goals had left behind more collateral damage than he intended, especially regarding relationships. Networking relationships were far fickler than he would have predicted. Also, his existing clients seemed to get in the way of attracting new ones. The professional yet personalized experience he had created was taking a hit, so referrals were dropping. He even began to lose clients - ouch! He'd worked tirelessly to build a healthy culture, but even the relationships of his team members had turned sour.

Adding the proverbial insult to injury, his family had decided to add to his stress during this low point with miscommunication and frustrations over minor issues. The arguments and frustrations outside the office made it more challenging to overcome the obstacles inside the office. As if these uphill challenges were insufficient, the cash flow was increasingly difficult to forecast.

Jacob knew he was not where he needed to be, and something had to change, or the consequences would be severe. Sensing he was close to burnout, he confessed inwardly, then to his wife, that his life was all out of order. He committed to getting his priorities in their proper order.

At the peak of his top-performing months, he had been recognized for outstanding achievements, but the most arduous struggle was putting his ego back in check. He no longer needed to be the best; he wanted balance. More than a position or profit, he desired peace. He prayed.

Jacob began to search for answers and committed to finding out how to manage his business instead of letting his business manage him. Knowing he couldn't fix his problems with the same mindset that created them, he looked for others who might help. Was there someone with an answer?

During his search, he stumbled upon coaching videos online that seemed inspirational and informational, touching both the head and the heart. This "Improver" concept was intriguing to Jacob as he usually came across heady and complicated content with no conviction and competing values. Often, it was information that was all fluff and hype with no actionable message.

When he dug further, the light bulb came on. He realized he was not alone and that many of his issues and battles are what every entrepreneur faces. He learned that errors and failures are indeed the standard price of admission for experiencing success. Having previously adopted the adage of "work hard, play hard" (much to his exhaustion), he would now add "work smart" to the mantra.

How would he "get smart?"

By consistently absorbing relevant content and making meaningful connections with a community of people on the same path as him. He decided to enlist a business coach who would offer real-time feedback on his processes and performance, using timeless growth and leadership principles.

The first thing the coach did was help Jacob focus on the good instead of only seeing what needed to get better. As he developed an attitude of gratitude, he experienced significant momentum around healthy habits and rhythms.

Jacob also made intentional decisions to add purposeful people to his inner circle, particularly other guys who would hold him accountable. The phrase "in business for yourself, but not by yourself" was starting to make sense.

Learning, improving, and adapting, it wasn't long before Jacob began to see new fruit. It wasn't always easy parsing through the various tools and concepts to figure out which ones were best suited for him and his practice, yet over time, the time distance between trying and succeeding narrowed. His network was expanding, his book of business was growing, and his impact was magnifying. He helped bring up individuals on his team and created incredible constructive collaboration among his growing company's different units and divisions.

Things were also more enjoyable at home. There were time and money margins and emotional bandwidth to share with family and friends. Travel and new experiences were no longer bucket list items; occurrences were growing in frequency. Although the storms still came, Jacob found they were easier to weather and didn't seem to last as long or be as damaging. The ever-elusive, thriving life of having peace while being present AND productive was no longer an aspiration – Jacob was living it. He now understood what it meant to live life as an Improver.

Another effect of having additional space in the calendar was the opportunity to spend more time in wonder and vision, extra moments to contemplate strategies and goals, and ponder what could and should be. During one of these imagination sessions, Jacob realized that as much as he enjoyed parts of his life, he received the most joy by investing in others. It dawned on him that he had spent his life chasing success. While success had its benefits, he longed for something greater—significance.

He reflected on how much he wanted his life to count and for people to remember him as positively impacting the world. He understood that helping people in their careers and growing teams was terrific, but the most significant impact he could make would be to develop more leaders to be Improvers like him.

Jacob began his transformation journey without apparent purpose and peace about life and business. Marked by feelings of insecurity and stagnation, unhealthy habits, and unproductive systems/processes, his impact on others fluctuated between non-existent and negative.

As an Improver, he now has a clear vision and direction, personally and professionally. He leveled up to feelings of significance and momentum, healthy habits and systems/processes, and high impact with others. Jacob's life trajectory had been improved. For him, he was a better person, and the world was a better place.

THIS BOOK

Although Jacob's story is fictional, Jacob's life change illustrates the desire of this book: to help you live intentionally as an Improver so you can experience positive change and make a meaningful impact on those around you. My objective was to enlighten you regarding what it means to be an Improver, encourage you to become one, and equip you with models and tools to assist you on your journey.

By taking on an identity as an Improver and embodying the mentality and attitudes of other Improvers, you'll avoid the pitfall of becoming an Exister or Diminisher, and instead find more life significance, inner peace, and unshakable joy.

I'm convinced that consistently living out the *Daily High Five* of showing thanks, growing healthy, living on purpose, being accountable, and serving others while keeping a mindset of hope, adaptability, faith-driven action, and integrity can change you for the better and improve the world.

OUR VISION, YOUR INVITATION

At Improver Group, the vision is to ignite a transformative movement that inspires 2.5 million people over the next ten years to commit to becoming an Improver.

By fostering a community of faith-driven individuals dedicated to personal development, service, and leadership at home and in the marketplace, we can create a ripple effect of positive growth and effective change.

Our movement of Improvers can (and will) help everyday people escape average, build a legacy of greatness, integrity, and compassion, and make a meaningful impact on our world.

If you resonate with this vision and the principles outlined in the Improver movement, I invite you to join us on this journey by agreeing to the following "I am an Improver" statement.

I commit to the journey of becoming an Improver and will strive to uphold the following principles and practices in my personal and professional life:

— **Improve Continuously:** I will embrace a mindset of continuous improvement, always looking for ways to learn, grow, and enhance my skills and knowledge.

- **Show Thanks:** I will cultivate a spirit of gratituce, recognizing the blessings and opportunities in my life, expressing appreciation to those around me, and being content (but not complacent) regardless of circumstances.
- **Grow Healthy:** I will prioritize my physical, mentcl, emotional, and spiritual well-being, proactively striving for balance and resilience in every key area of my life.
- **Be on Purpose:** I will pursue my goals with intention and clarity, aligning my actions with my true purpose and long-term vision.
- **Be Accountable:** I will enlist others in my inner circle to hold me acccuntable, ensuring I stay true to my values, responsibilities, and commitments.
- **Serve Others:** I wil look for opportunities to serve and uplift others, conributing to their growth and well-being with generosity and compassion.
- **Cultivate Potential:** I will actively seek and nurture the potential within myself and others, fostering a supportive and encouraging environment guided by faith and hope
- **Win with Integrity:** I will strive for success with integrity, demonstrating ethcal behavior and inspiring others through my commitment to moral principles.

I acknowledge my commitment to the journey of becoming an Improver and my dedication to making a positive impact on the world.

If you are making this commitment to become an Improver and join the movement, please let us know by visiting: www.improverchallenge.com.

APPENDIX

APPENDIX A: PRAYER OF THE IMPROVER

Heavenly Father, I praise You for Your greatness and wisdom. None is greater than You.

You are completely good, and You are working all things together for good. You are in control.

Thank You for all that You have provided for me.

Thank You for Your love, grace, and the strength to overcome challenges.

Forgive me for my complacency and moments of drift.

Help me improve continuously, always seeking to learn, grow, and enhance my skills for Your kingdom.

Cultivate in me a spirit of gratitude, recognizing blessings and opportunities, and expressing appreciation to those around me.

Guide me to grow healthy in every area of my life, balancing physical, mental, emotional, and spiritual well-being.

Grant me the clarity to be on purpose, aligning my actions with Your vision and plan for my life.

Keep me accountable to You and others, ensuring I stay true to my convictions and commitments.

Empower me to serve others, contributing to their growth with generosity and compassion.

Help me cultivate potential within myself and others, fostering a supportive environment guided by faith and hope.

Enable me today to rise above mediocrity and fulfill the greatness You have placed within me, striving for success with integrity and inspiring others through my commitment to Your word.

In your name, I pray. Amen.

APPENDIX B: 40-DAY CHALLENGE

⚡ IMPROVER 40-DAY CHALLENGE

ONE-TIME TASKS

- [ ] ACCEPT THE IMPROVER CHALLENGE ONLINE
- [ ] DRAFT (1-3) F.A.S.T. GOALS
- [ ] ENLIST ACCOUNTABILITY PARTNER OR COACH

WEEKLY PLANNING

	1	2	3	4	5	6
RECORD YOUR WINS						
WRITE YOUR BIG 3						

DAILY ACTION

WEEK 1	MON	TUE	WED	THU	FRI	SAT	SUN
PLAN ACTION ITEMS							
SHOW THANKS							
SERVE SOMEONE							

WEEK 2	MON	TUE	WED	THU	FRI	SAT	SUN
PLAN ACTION ITEMS							
SHOW THANKS							
SERVE SOMEONE							

WEEK 3	MON	TUE	WED	THU	FRI	SAT	SUN
PLAN ACTION ITEMS							
SHOW THANKS							
SERVE SOMEONE							

WEEK 4	MON	TUE	WED	THU	FRI	SAT	SUN
PLAN ACTION ITEMS							
SHOW THANKS							
SERVE SOMEONE							

WEEK 5	MON	TUE	WED	THU	FRI	SAT	SUN
PLAN ACTION ITEMS							
SHOW THANKS							
SERVE SOMEONE							

WEEK 6	MON	TUE	WED	THU	FRI	SAT	SUN
PLAN ACTION ITEMS							
SHOW THANKS							
SERVE SOMEONE							

ENDNOTES

1. Merriam-Webster. (n.d.). Exister. In Merriam-Webster.com dictionary. Retrieved from https://www.merriam-webster.com
2. Kennedy, R. F., Jr. (2023). Interview with Dr. Drew Pinsky. Retrieved from Dr. Drew Official Website.
3. Lencioni, P. (2016). The Ideal Team Player: How to Recognize and Cultivate the Three Essential Virtues. Jossey-Bass
4. Holy Bible, Christian Standard Bible. Nashville: Holman Bible Publishers, 2017. Matthew 5:13-16
5. Frankl, V. E. (2006). Man's Search for Meaning. Beacon Press.
6. Allen, James. As a Man Thinketh. Project Gutenberg, 1903.
7. Holy Bible, Christian Standard Bible. Nashville: Holman Bible Publishers, 2017. Matthew 7:5.
8. Ziglar, Zig. See You at the Top. Pelican Publishing, 2000.
9. Perry, M. (2022). Friends, Lovers, and the Big Terrible Thing: A Memoir. Flatiron Books.
10. Lencioni, P. (2020). The 6 Types of Working Genius: A Better Way to Understand Your Gifts, Your Frustrations, and Your Team. Table Group.
11. Zander, Benjamin, and Rosamund Stone Zander. The Art of Possibility: Transforming Professional and Personal Life. Harvard Business School Press, 2000.
12. Robbins, Mel. The High 5 Habit: Take Control of Your Life with One Simple Habit. Hay House, 2021
13. The New York Times. (2016, October 27). For Real, the Close Door Button in Your Elevator May Not Work. Retrieved from https://www.nytimes.com/2016/10/28/nyregion/for-real-the-close-door-button-in-your-elevator-may-not-work.html
14. BBC Future. (2019, April 1). The Pedestrian Push Button: A Short History of a Myth. Retrieved from https://www.bbc.com/future/article/20190327-the-pedestrian-push-button-a-short-history-of-a-myth
15. Sullivan, D., & Hardy, B. (2021). The Gap and The Gain: The High Achievers' Guide to Happiness, Confidence, and Success. Hay House Inc.

16. Acuff, J. (2017). Finish: Give Yourself the Gift of Done. Penguin Publishing Group.
17. Cinderella. "Don't Know What You Got (Till It's Gone)." Long Cold Winter, Mercury Records, 1988.
18. Holy Bible, Christian Standard Bible. Nashville: Holman Bible Publishers, 2017. Philippians 4:11-13.
19. Holy Bible, English Standard Version. Wheaton: Crossway Bibles, 2001. 1 Thessalonians 5:18.
20. Holy Bible, New Living Translation. Carol Stream: Tyndale House Publishers, 2015. Ephesians 5:20.
21. Robinson, R. (1758). Come Thou Fount of Every Blessing.
22. Searcy, Nelson. The Renegade Pastor: Abandoning Average in Your Life and Ministry. Baker Books, 2013.
23. Wikipedia. (n.d.). SMART criteria. Retrieved from https://en.wikipedia.org/wiki/SMART_criteria
24. Holy Bible, Contemporary English Version. New York: American Bible Society, 1995. Proverbs 21:5.
25. Holy Bible, Christian Standard Bible. Nashville: Holman Bible Publishers, 2017. Psalm 139:13-16.
26. Holy Bible, New Living Translation. Carol Stream: Tyndale House Publishers, 2015. Ephesians 2:10.
27. Holy Bible, New International Version. (1978). Proverbs 19:21. Zondervan
28. Holy Bible, GOD'S WORD Translation. Grand Rapids: Baker Publishing Group, 1995. 2 Corinthians 9:8.
29. Holy Bible, Christian Standard Bible. Nashville: Holman Bible Publishers, 2017. Matthew 6:25-33.
30. Holy Bible, Christian Standard Bible. Nashville: Holman Bible Publishers, 2017. Philippians 4:6-7.
31. Holy Bible, New Living Translation. Carol Stream: Tyndale House Publishers, 2015. John 14:27.
32. Holy Bible, Christian Standard Bible. Nashville: Holman Bible Publishers, 2017. 2 Thessalonians 3:3.
33. Holy Bible, New International Version. (1978). Romans 8:28. Zondervan
34. Holy Bible, Christian Standard Bible. Nashville: Holman Bible Publishers, 2017. 2 Corinthians 12:9.

35. Holy Bible, New International Version. (1978). Ephesians 3:20. Zondervan

36. Holy Bible, New International Version. (1978). John 14:16-17. Zondervan

37. Holy Bible, Christian Standard Bible. Nashville: Holman Bible Publishers, 2017. Hebrews 13:5.

38. Coleman, K. (2019). The Proximity Principle: The Proven Strategy That Will Lead to a Career You Love. Ramsey Press.

39. Holy Bible, New International Version. (1978). Proverbs 24:5. Zondervan.

40. Saban, N. (2018). How Good Do You Want to Be? A Champion's Tips on How to Lead and Succeed. Ballantine Books.

41. Pascal, Blaise. De l'Art de persuader. 1658. Published posthumously.

42. Acuff, J. (2021). Soundtracks: The Surprising Solution to Overthinking. Baker Books.

43. Holy Bible, Christian Standard Bible. Nashville: Holman Bible Publishers, 2017. Matthew 6:22

44. Tolkien, J. R. R. The Fellowship of the Ring. George Allen & Unwn, 1954.

45. Cron, I. M., & Stabile, S. (2016). The Road Back to You: An Enneagram Journey to Self-Discovery. InterVarsity Press.

46. Holy Bible, Holman Christian Standard Bible. Nashville: Holman Bible Publishers, 2009. Philippians 2:3-4. (Emphasis mine.)

47. Ziglar, Z. (2007). Secrets of Closing the Sale. Revell.

48. Carnegie, Dale. How to Win Friends and Influence People. New York: Simon and Schuster, 1936.

49. Gabhart, K. (2023). Legends Don't Retire: How to Live Your Legacy and Lead a Life that Matters. (p.65-66). Bluegrass Legacy Group.

50. Holy Bible, Christian Standard Bible. Nashville: Holman Bible Publishers, 2017. Matthew 20:28.

51. Holy Bible, Christian Standard Bible. Nashville: Holman Bible Publishers, 2017. Philippians 4:13.

52. Aristotle. (2007). On Rhetoric: A Theory of Civic Discourse (G. A. Kennedy, Trans.). Oxford University Press.

53. Giglio, L. (2013). Passion: The Bright Light of Glory. Thomas Nelson.

54. Stanley, C. F. (2008). In Touch with God: How God Speaks to You and Transforms Your Life. Howard Books.

55. *Shark Tank*. Created by Mark Burnett, ABC, 2009-present.
56. Tracy, B. (2001). The 100 Absolutely Unbreakable Laws of Business Success. Berrett-Koehler Publishers.
57. Johnson, S. (1998). Who Moved My Cheese? An Amazing Way to Deal with Change in Your Work and in Your Life. G.P. Putnam's Sons.
58. Stanley PMI. (2023). Stanley Brand Story. Retrieved from https://www.stanley1913.com/pages/our-brand
59. Thau, Barbara. "10X Sales Increase: What Every Business Can Learn From the Stanley Tumbler Phenomenon." U.S. Chamber of Commerce, 2024.
60. Redding, D. (2023). QSource: The F3 Manual of Virtuous Leadership. F3 Nation.
61. Maslow, A. H. (1987). Motivation and Personality. Harper & Row.
62. Twain, M. (1993). Mark Twain's Own Autobiography: The Chapters from the North American Review. University of Wisconsin Press
63. University of New Hampshire. (2021). Conspiracy vs. Science: A Survey of U.S. Public Beliefs. Carsey School of Public Policy. Retrieved from https://carsey.unh.edu/publication/conspiracy-vs-science
64. Ziglar, T. (2019). Choose to Win: Transform Your Life, One Simple Choice at a Time. Thomas Nelson.
65. Ramsey, D. (2009). The Total Money Makeover: A Proven Plan for Financial Fitness. Thomas Nelson.
66. Keller, H. (1994). The Story of My Life. Dover Publications.
67. London, J. (1903). The Call of the Wild. Macmillan.
68. London, J. (1913). Letter to Philo Buck. In The Letters of Jack London (Vol. 2, pp. 185-186). Stanford University Press.
69. Holy Bible, Christian Standard Bible. Nashville: Holman Bible Publishers, 2017. Matthew 25:21.
70. Holy Bible, Christian Standard Bible. Nashville: Holman Bible Publishers, 2017. James 2:26.
71. Austen, Jane. Pride and Prejudice. Public Domain. Chapter 31.
72. Indiana Jones and the Last Crusade. Directed by Steven Spielberg, performances by Harrison Ford and Sean Connery, Paramount Pictures, 1989.

73. Thoreau, H. D. (1857). Letter to H.G.O. Blake, 1857. In H. G. O. Blake (Ed.), Letters to a Spiritual Seeker (pp. 181-182). W.W. Norton & Company.
74. Hyatt, M. (2020). Free to Focus: A Total Productivity System to Achieve More by Doing Less. Baker Books.
75. Holy Bible, New International Version. (1978). Proverbs 31:16-27. Zondervan.
76. Wordsworth, W. (n.d.). To begin, begin. Retrieved from https://www.poetryfoundation.org/poets/william-wordsworth
77. Burton, P. (1958). Red Alert. Vantage Press.

INDEX

www.ingramcontent.com/pod-product-compliance
Lightning Source LLC
Chambersburg PA
CBHW021139130626
46554CB00005B/1583